SHADOWS IN THE TWILIGHT

CONVERSATIONS WITH A SHAMAN

By

LUJAN MATUS & W. L. HAM

Disclaimer

The author specifically disclaims any responsibility for any liability, loss, or risk, personal or otherwise, which is incurred as a consequence, directly or indirectly, of the use and application of any of the contents of this book.

ISBN: 1470063247

ISBN 13: 9781470063245

With deep thanks to all
who lovingly contributed
to the editing process:

Sugrue
Phe Gitsham
Luma Chichiwa
Ben Chandler
Gordon Fry
& Lyra

SPECIAL THANKS TO:

W. L. Ham
Naomi Jean
Levent Kecik
& to my beautiful wife
Mizpah Matus.

AN OLD CHEROKEE ONCE TOLD HIS GRANDSON:

"My son, inside us all
there is a battle between two wolves.
One is Evil. It is anger, jealousy, greed,
arrogance, resentment, inferiority, lies, and ego.
The other is Good. It is joy, peace, love,
hope, humility, kindness, empathy, and truth."
The grandson thought about it for a minute
and then asked his grandfather:
"Which wolf wins?"
The wise man quietly replied,
"The one you feed."

NATIVE AMERICAN PROVERB

TABLE OF CONTENTS

Introduction xi
Glossary xiii
The Man in the Hat 1
Generations 9
They Bite 16
Crossing Over 26
Continuum: Encounters and Origins 31
Dreams and Visions 34
Energetic Anchoring 40
Resonance 46
Remote Viewing, Dreaming and The Photonic Eye 49
Waiting 68
Love and Lust 71
Twilight 75
Memory 77
Witnessing the Double 79
Encounters with the Nagual's Double 83
The Next Afternoon 89
Night Gazing Session One 91
Night Gazing Session Two 93

The Next Day: Lessons in Absorbing Silence . . . 95
Times of Great Sorrow . . . 97
Natural Remote Viewing . . . 99
Confidence . . . 103
Reincarnation as a Dimensional Shift . . . 109
Light Filaments . . . 119
The Round Shadow . . . 121
Different Types of Seeing . . . 126
The World as a Mirror . . . 130
Communication . . . 139
Stalking . . . 142
Teachers and Benefactors . . . 145
Crackling Beings . . . 147
The Heart of Hearts . . . 163
Everyday Entrapments . . . 166
Hearing is for Seeing . . . 174
Cloaked . . . 176
Installed Fixations . . . 177
Mescalito . . . 180
Human Connectivity and Non-Sequential Time . . . 183
Reincarnation of the Old Nagual Lujan . . . 187
Looking for the Hands in Dreaming . . . 196
Lujan's Double . . . 200
Human Potential vs. Predatorial Projections . . . 202
Reclamation . . . 209
Possession . . . 213
Unfathomable Equations . . . 216
The Universal Equalizer . . . 222
Epilogue . . . 227
The Mirror . . . 228

With this book I beckon the memory of our future,
which we have already visited,
to be awakened in the mysteries of our moment
that we patiently await to appear.

LUJAN MATUS

INTRODUCTION

My name is Bill. I have studied the path of the warrior, and shamanism in general, for many years. I have read, many times, the works of all the most popular authors and leaders in this field. I felt that I had a pretty good grip on the information.

I was online one day looking for new material, when I came across a book titled 'The Art of Stalking Parallel Perception'. I read it and read it again. This book began to challenge what I had already learned. One day I was thumbing through the pages, when I realized there was a website in the back of the book: www.parallelperception.com. I followed the link and found the shaman Nagual Lujan Matus. I interacted with him and other practitioners of his teachings in his online forum and, after about a year, I became one of Lujan's students. This began with conversations over the phone, since Lujan was not in the same part of the world as I was at that time.

We spoke like this for about two years before I was able to travel to meet and study with him personally. I have been his student now for some years and in recent months Lujan has allowed me to record our conversations. This is how this book has come to be. It is a glimpse into some of what Lujan has taught me in my apprenticeship with him. In some cases, these conversations start with me telling a story and then Lujan speaking to what he sees in my story. In other instances the subjects naturally present themselves to be explored.

If you find some of the material difficult to comprehend, don't let it worry you. It takes a certain amount of a person's energy to be able to assimilate new information, so if you notice yourself getting confused, it may be that you don't yet have the energetic speed to grasp the vastness of what is being introduced. It has been years now that I have been absorbing these teachings and I am still discovering new complexities within the subjects.

If a concept doesn't come to you immediately, or you don't see the application, give it time to unfold. Apply what you can and you will begin to store energy. As your energy grows, so will your capacity to comprehend. I have found many times in my conversations with the Nagual that I don't understand what I am being shown until I find a reference point in my life. Then suddenly the information rushes in and I realize what he has taught me. Be patient with yourself and you will see that more is close at hand than you may realize.

GLOSSARY

Usually a glossary is included at the back of a book to provide simple definitions of specialized terminology. I am purposely diverging away from this convention so as to give the reader an in-depth explanation of interchangeable descriptions that embody actual contradictions, as can only be experienced by a warrior on their life path.

What everybody will be subject to through reading 'Shadows in the Twilight' is the 'mirror neuron' effect, from a shamanic perspective, which naturally goes beyond an anthropological standpoint. To illustrate, when one monkey observes another in motion, what is witnessed is then learned, through the process of being seen. What I would like to elucidate here is the fact that something much deeper than mere absorption of the observable phenomenon is occurring.

A purely Cartesian approach becomes a virtual façade, stilting humanity's perceptual growth via its absolutism. When this system is taken literally, the intuitive world of the warrior is entirely left out of the equation. Upon this premise, perception is solidified through the process of reasonable understanding, which gives rise to specific ideas that do not take into consideration the innumerable subatomic phylums witnessed which deliver content randomly in correspondence with the perceiver's capacity to understand throughout their lifetime.

For example, when one gazes at a star, the influx of information that is obtained by a shaman is more than the visual composite of data that scientists have categorized as a fixed perception, in terms of what can be understood and verified, in comparison to the object being witnessed.

When a shaman gazes, they irrefutably know that what comes upon them through that practice will contain more than what is visually apprehended from a rational perspective. As this absorption applies its pressure upon the energetic configuration of the witness, a multiplex of factors come into play. Thus the seer begins to notice that they know more than what they expected, by virtue of the fact that they expect nothing from the initial act, inevitably nullifying the need to categorize. This book is an act within itself to allow this process to occur, through the explanations outlined.

The first attention is the basic reality that we live within, our waking world, which in essence, from a shaman's perspective, holds the key to all that is, in terms of what is not obviously available; the mystery of life itself.

The second attention is where we enter into dreams and experience similar phenomena: A world that appears to deliver coherency, in spite of its elusive nature, and which holds within its vastness secrets that are highly sought after by ancient and modern shamans alike.

The third attention is the combination of the previous two. It is where the visual matrix of the first attention becomes intermixed with random imagery that appears as holographic units of information to be witnessed, superimposed within our waking world.

The fourth attention is where, through acts of power, a seer will draw to themselves the exact duplicate of their physical form, The Double, integrated within the first attention matrix, activating second attention capacity, through to a third attention ability to interdimensionally interchange past, present, and future corresponding parallel universes, which are simultaneously witnessed, as our ability to internally galactically align with our truest path as human beings.

THE MAN IN THE HAT

I had been out hunting deer with a good friend of mine all afternoon. As the sun set, we were still a good distance away from any civilization, in the depths of our swampy hunting ground. In the weeks before I had been reading many of the works of a well-known author on the subject of sorcery and shamanism, and my mind was fertile for any sort of 'sign' or signal from the world at large. As I waited alone for my friend to return to our woody meeting place, I sat on a log, noticing that the darkness of night seemed to be borne from the depths of the forest itself. There was just a touch of blue left in the sky as I sat waiting.

Suddenly, I noticed a large bird swoop overhead. It was nothing more than a black silhouette on the azure sky. Normally, this would not have even caught my attention, except for the fact that I am very familiar with the birds in the area and this did not fit the behavior and description of any of the birds I knew. Since it was almost dark, I thought that it was not likely to be a hawk, or the rare eagle.

"They roost before the sky is at this point," I said out loud, not really sure who would be listening.

"Not an owl," I continued, "because that was easily twice the size of any of the largest owls in the area. Not a vulture; they're scavengers and don't look for food near dark."

At this point, my mind began to revert to what I had been reading during the weeks before. It must be an omen or a sign of some kind! So I did what anyone would do in near-dark swamp far from any city. I went to see what it was. I started in the direction the bird seemed to be flying in. I say 'seemed' because it vanished as fast as it appeared, almost as if it were a shadow. I began walking north, not really sure of what I was looking for or what a sign or an omen would look like, even if it were something of that nature. I had gone about one hundred yards deeper into the woods when I found what I was searching for.

As I stared, I was instantly frozen with fear; not the kind of fear you have when something startles you or a friend sneaks up behind you to play a joke. I was literally immobilized. This was fear that can only be realized in the body, not in the mind. About thirty more paces in front of me was a man. He was perfectly still, but seemed to be stepping out from behind a tree. In the fading light, he was not much more than a black silhouette. He wore a large-brimmed hat and his head was tilted slightly forward. I could just make out the glint of one eye peering at me from beneath the rim. My mind went as numb as my body. After a few seconds, my brain kicked back in and the internal dialogue started back up.

"What the hell is that?! It's a man, you damn fool. The hell it is! I know a man when I see one and that is not a man. Okay, shoot him. Then what?! I can't shoot him. Why, you got a gun? Shoot him! What should a warrior do? Tackle him! Okay, now you're really nuts. Yep, that's what you got to do, run over there and tackle him. If it's one of those ally things, you've got to wrestle it to the ground. Here goes!"

With that, I let out the fiercest yell I could and rushed forward. I figured if it was some old farmer or psychokiller we were about to settle up. If it was an entity of the type that I had read about, then my plan was to forcibly tackle it. The stories I had read said that young shaman waited and wandered deep in the wilderness at night until being confronted by one of these creatures. The idea was that if you could physically subdue it, then you would be able to take control of it and it would then serve you with a gift of power or knowledge. Sounded good at the time, so off I went to do battle with this shadow man!

No sooner than I had taken about half a step, the true identity of the man was revealed: An old stump and a shadow cast from a nearby branch had created the illusion of a man stepping out from behind a tree. Even to this day, I am not sure if I was relieved or disappointed. I stood there looking at what my body still knew was not a man nor an illusion, but something in between, something else. My rational mind eventually took over and I laughed the entire event off. Of course I had been reading too much of this sorcery nonsense and my mind was now playing tricks on me, right?

Not long afterward, my friend came wandering back to camp. "What the hell y'all doing all that yelling for?"

"Stumped my toe."

I forgot about this event for some time. But this would not be my first encounter with something of this nature. One can only dismiss these things as fantasy for so long. Some years later, I realized a pattern and an increasing frequency in such events. This is when I began relaying my stories to Lujan for review.

Bill:

Was what I saw a real entity or my imagination?

Lujan:

What you saw was a second attention anomaly, which is an aspect of dreaming awareness. As soon as it became recognizable in the first attention, which is your 'normal', everyday awareness in the waking world, it vanished. As far as the first attention is concerned, it didn't happen. As for the second attention, it did.

Bill:

Why was I scared of it?

Lujan:

This entity is not what you think. It's an embodiment of the peyote plant. I came across Mescalito forty years ago, but it was not me who saw him. At that time in my life, he was a protector of sorts.

Bill:

That doesn't make any sense.

Lujan:

It does. There were people in my house at the time and they encountered him and told me about it. When they relayed the story to me, I saw the man through their vision, in the same way he came to me through yours. This is what I meant when I said your experience was a facet of the second attention. Those scenes were embedded with information that I was able to understand when I gazed into them. What I saw was that he was protecting these people. The fact that he came to me through their vision is how I knew of my connection to them; in the same way I now know how I am connected to you. This is how the ally has shown itself to me, but never directly, only through the eyes of those he points out.

Bill:

I'm still not sure I understand what you are saying. Why would this thing show up in the woods and scare the shit out of me like that? Was I in danger of this creature?

Lujan:

(Now laughing out loud.) No, you weren't in any danger, but that's not the point at all. You were able to dream in the waking world. Your third eye was unveiled and you were seeing, in true second attention. This means you have taken the context of your visual reality, which manifests as a holographic scene in dreams, and transported it into the waking world as units of information that contain wisdom pertinent to the level of personal power you have obtained thus far. This is the beginning of the worldly manifestations of the third attention.

The point is that, for you, it was only a snapshot of that world. As soon as your rational mind and your social conditioning jumped back in, the man in the hat became a branch and a shadow again. You have not rid yourself of your programming enough to maintain the second attention view. Maintaining that view is how I see the man in your vision, and how I can lend my voice to the scene and speak the information embedded in it.

The accounts of ancient sorcerers attempting to subdue inorganic entities within the first attention led you to believe that you should have tackled the man in the hat. This information has caused significant confusion, as it cannot be applied in a blanket sense to all phenomena that manifest outside the socially-accepted parameters of normalcy. You assumed that the man in the hat was the same kind of entity described in the books that introduced you to these possibilities. When faced with this encounter, you blindly mimicked what had been outlined. If your body consciousness had taken over, instead of your mind, the outcome would have been different.

In fact, the man in the hat is the entity known as Mescalito, whom the ancient sorcerers would have recognized as a personification of a hallucinogenic spirit, which does not appear in order to entice you into second attention fixations. Unlike Mescalito, most apparitions of this kind are mere probes that embody the electrical impulse of their inorganic source-emitter. When that charge gets transferred to the warrior's bio-electromagnetic field through the contact, this can be sufficient to establish the hook necessary to lure awareness into the second attention, which, in essence, is the non-locatable base of operations for inorganic beings. For us, it is a predatorial domain in that it is inhabited by entities that sustain themselves on photonic energy, of which we represent a resource.

Once a warrior becomes energetically aligned with these influences, there is a great risk to be trapped in the second attention; an unknown territory where one can spend a lifetime wandering labyrinths and getting absorbed emotionally in memories and reference points that will never be resolved. Little did the ancient sorcerers know that, in this way, they were being coercively maneuvered, bit by bit, away from their heart path.

What those seers persistently focused on throughout their life was to develop the capacity to transport their photonic eye to altered states, which are in reality interdimensional dreaming shifts. In other words, after seeing something like the ally, they would have tried to pursue it in lucid dreaming, which as you know is the second attention.

Seers were led to believe, via the feelings obtained on those dreaming journeys, that their power revealed itself as a scene to interact within. As the old sorcerers became accustomed to these scenes, they gained the potency of that familiarity. What they didn't realize is that by entering into this inorganic symbiosis, they were merging with a frequency that would ultimately withdraw its contact at the moment of their death. When one's energy is reclaimed at this crucial juncture, the photonic potential of the warrior, which contains the memories of their journey, is possessed and becomes absolutely inaccessible; thus nullifying the seer's ability to bring back these source points of information, as emanations of light, to nourish their own inner matrix. This is why Juan Matus described the second attention fixation as a dead end pursuit.

In spite of the abundant information that can be gained in exchange for one's precious photonic energy, the drawback is that, while reasonable knowledge is made available, abstract wisdom is never fully arrived upon. The ongoing drain of our essential energy into persuasively reasonable premises is one of the traps that cordons a warrior off from their heart path and conceals their true potential.

Bill:

Why were they so focused on the second attention? Were they seeking power?

Lujan:

Yes. The grave mistake they made was that the power they sought was to be found here, by accessing the third attention through the first attention matrix.

Bill:

The third? I'm still stuck working on the second.

Lujan:

Exactly my point. You must access the third attention by bringing your dreaming awareness, or your second attention, to this world, the first attention. The key is not to seek to go into dreaming with agendas. Bringing your photonic perceptual capacity to manifest here is the third attention. This is how you will become an awakened seer. The old sorcerers used their dreaming to hunt and endeavor to possess the power they sought. The new seers do not seek to control this power. We become the power itself, by virtue of the fact that we do not seek it. This is a primary hinge point of the not-doing of power.

Bill:

I'm not sure I know how to maintain the second attention here like that. Why is it so fleeting? Is it because I don't have enough power yet?

If I had more energy, could I have maintained the vision longer, or even indefinitely? Could I have run over there and actually tackled the ally?

Lujan:

Look what you are doing now. You are reciting the old sorcerers' way verbatim. By doing this you change your second attention view into a first attention expectation, and the vision fades due to you trying to emulate someone else's experience with the whole tackling thing. You lose your sustainable potency, for it is no longer your story. Now you have an expectation of what your experience is and what it should be, or what the man in the hat should do. That's programming.

You are trying to catch power with the same old hook and the same old bait. You can't have a hook and you can't have bait. So many people do this very same thing. They read about sorcery and believe they have power because they attempt to replicate the journey of another. They're nothing more than paper tigers.

You will now have to wait until power presents itself again. Next time, try not to allow your programming or your expectations to jump in. Be clear of mind and heart, and let the event be what it will be. This is how to lay the groundwork for the second attention to arrive in the daytime reality and allow your awareness to be encompassed by more than what you think you know.

Bill:

I think I understand. The vision faded not because of a lack of power so much as because of expectations created from what I thought I knew. I should not have met the vision with beliefs or programming, and least of all with someone else's ideas. I should have silenced my mind and maintained the scene by bringing my dreaming attention here to the first attention.

Lujan:

Right. The vision faded because the programming that you have inherited took over. This social conditioning is unwittingly handed down to young children from their parents and their peers. If something like the man in the hat had shown itself to you as a child, you would have told your parents. And what would they have said to you? "Oh, how cute. What an imagination." They would not have believed you. Eventually, you would have to conform to this worldview to fit into society. This is how we lose our access to our true ability to see.

In that state, you can't see anything magical. Everything you see becomes social. Anything that comes at you must fit into the accepted description you have been taught. That's why the man in the hat became a branch. You adapted what you saw to accommodate your social programming, which would not allow the existence of an entity like that, and he obliged by disappearing.

The message in the scene for you personally was that you have enough power to go beyond what you are.

You can experience your dreams externally, but if your scripted responses get in the way, all there will be are branches and shadows in your life, nothing more. The real magic is right in front of our eyes all the time, but we must wait until it avails itself to us. Eventually all of us will see the magic through what presents itself in the moment that immediately escapes us. People try to force their way through. Here is where seers get off track. You can't force these things. When it's appropriate, you can see through the veil. When it's not appropriate, there is nothing to be seen. Here is where you have to wait for your inevitability to confront you with a gift of eternity.

Bill:

Well then, what do we do with what we see?

Lujan:

You use it as the verification that your imagery is becoming so strong that you're beginning to pierce through the veil of the third eye. These are the tools of power that are there for you to use here, as a human being. This is how we progress. Slowly we witness our second attention imagery appearing externally. Power and information is available to a seer in these images.

GENERATIONS

Let me tell you a story, Bill. My mother died the other night. She didn't really have much input in my life since the time when I was a young boy, but when I got the email that she was dying, I decided to get in touch and bid her farewell while she was still alive. I didn't get the chance. She died before I was able to make contact with her.

About a day after her death, I felt her being hovering around me making one last visitation whilst within dreaming. Now, what you need to know is that I don't have random dreams when I sleep. When I do dream, the images are filled with information that is absolutely pertinent to what I need to realize. So the other night when she came to me just after she died, I knew it was a genuine visitation.

Even though it was the essential essence of her being that came to me, she herself was unaware of that unifying act. She didn't have the power to be cognizant of the full ramifications of the traversing of her own death, yet the gravity of my being drew her to me, so as to bring closure to our karmic connection.

I saw her laying in her bed dying, and next to her lay her husband who had died many years before. I was witness to the energetic consequences of their conjoining in bardo. I knew they couldn't see me, yet the act itself gave my being the opportunity to convey my thanks for their input in certain circumstances in my youth. Although it was unspoken, the message was energetically transmitted, thus severing the etheric threads that bound us.

Bill:

That's startling. My grandmother went into a stroke-induced coma less than a week ago. She could not speak or communicate with anyone. I had a dream two nights ago. In the dream, I came to her bed. My family was in the room, trying to speak to her, and they could not make her hear them. I took her hand in mine and she was able to speak to me alone. I said goodbye and thank you. Unlike your mother, she had had a tremendous effect on my life in a wonderful way.

Lujan:

That's not an ordinary dream. It's something else.

Bill:

What is it then?

Lujan:

It's a true dreaming experience. The ancient shamans were masters of saying thank you and goodbye. They always stopped and bid farewell to the land when they left an area. They were never sure if they would be able to return in life to do this, but they knew for certain they would return in death to say their final goodbyes. They were attempting to preempt the moment of their death by performing this ritual, so as to obtain all the embedded information that they would absorb at the moment of their inevitable end. Such behavior is more symbolic than anything, for you can't really procure what you want no matter what you do. Ultimately we get what we need.

If a seer is habitually fixated on ritualistic behavior, he or she will not have the fluidity to discover the magic that awaits them at the end of their life.

In the case of your grandmother, she was truly saying goodbye, for it was her death she was speaking to, through you. This is the same thing that happened to me when I said goodbye to my mother. It was a genuine moment for us both.

There was one gesture that came from my mother that procured the outcome of my true destiny, which had enough power to allow me to say thank you at the moment of her death. That single event was the only thing I was actually saying goodbye to. Releasing anything else through this recognition would have been not only hypocrisy, but impossible to achieve within the vision, since it would have been absolutely energetically inappropriate.

It is through these kinds of experiences that a warrior begins to acknowledge the multifaceted factors that one directly realizes in the second attention, thus learning to apply this way of being as the ultimate energetic propriety in the first attention. Here one truly connects to Spirit through the gestures portrayed, which are enactments of integrity.

(At this point in our conversation, I began explaining to Lujan that I did not understand some of the ideas he was conveying with the story of his mother. He paused for a moment after hearing my complaints. I am always a little nervous when Lujan pauses in the middle of telling me something because I know he is 'seeing' and I'm never quite sure what's coming next.)

Lujan:

Bill, you're really an interesting character.

Bill:

That doesn't sound good.

Lujan:

I just explained to you the power of your attention. Listening to me tell the story of my mother was an absolute mirror image reflection of you relating to me your experience of the ally behind the tree. While I spoke and you gave me your attention, I realized deeper facets of what I saw. The difference between you and I is that you don't access the hidden treasures within your own journey when you share it. There is something that blocks you from your own realizations and steals your power in this world as a seer.

Bill:

Okay, I can understand that. But now my question is: What is the thing that is stealing my power? I need to turn and confront this thing to regain my place as a seer, but I don't know what it is.

Lujan:

It's your own idea of yourself, your absolute certainty of your own limitations. When I told the story of my mother, you believed it was a continuation of what I had realized when I first said goodbye. But that's not the whole truth. Through telling you, the power of my seeing became stronger, since you were also seeing my dream. As I described to you what had happened, you saw her and her husband lying in bed, didn't you?

Bill:

Yes, I did.

Lujan:

And I saw the image of the ally as you relayed the story to me. Your seeing became my seeing. The difference is, I understood the image and you don't believe you understood it. I don't pursue the need to understand, but when I see, I do understand. You don't allow yourself enough time to receive the information, as you attempt to force comprehension. You can't do that; you have to wait for it to arrive.

The second attention appearing in this first attention world gives me volumes of information. I then transfer this back to you as a form of insight that is heightened by our communal understanding, through the energy generated by our conversations. I can travel upon your vision because I believe in myself and I have no doubts in you.

The danger is when a teacher has doubts. If a teacher has misgivings about himself or herself, the student will inadvertently become caught in that maelstrom. If I believe in myself, I will see what you saw. Our attentions will link and interweave. When our visions merge in this manner, we are sharing a second attention dream scene. This communal connectivity is how we bring the vision of the world up to a higher level.

Bill:

I would like to slightly change the subject now. I have a question about something I was reading on your forum the other day. One of the people there was discussing the wind. He seemed to indicate that the wind was evil or dangerous and could cause illness. Is the wind evil?

Lujan:

No. But if you want to know something about what someone else said, you need to ask them directly. You are asking me to speak to someone else's insights and I can't do that. I can only speak from my own heart about my own experiences.

Bill:

Okay. But he also mentioned wind entities. This conversation is about entities, so can you tell me about things that may live in the wind? Other sorcery works have discussed such entities living in the wind. What is your opinion on that?

Lujan:

This is not going to work, Bill. What you are doing is trying to fish for a subject to discuss instead of being in the subject matter of your own life. What you have to do is allow the question to come out of yourself and the interpretation will occur as a natural transmission. You can't get transmission by asking questions that have no relevance to your own life at this particular moment. There is no point fishing with topics that have no meaning for you, for there is no real energy behind the inquiry. There will never be a real answer, since these are dead questions. It has to come from something alive within you, not something intellectually projected. I cannot speak with power to a subject that has no power.

The onus is on you to ask questions about your own experiences, like the story you told me about in the beginning of our conversation. That story was real and the power in it allowed you to transmit the visual image to me directly, and to that I spoke.

Bill:

Okay. I think I understand. The questions I was asking were stemming from my programming again. I was using my intellect, not my heart, from which to speak. Our life experiences live in our heart, as does as our power. This is why you have taught me to speak from the heart.

Lujan:

That's right. When speaking from the heart, one is automatically immersed in the field of intuitive immediacy.

Bill:

Could you elaborate?

Lujan:

Communication derived from outside our empathetic field is often borne from reason, which is just social and repetitive and dishonors the truth of the circumstance by bypassing the essence of the moment that exists. You must wait for the feeling of your inner voice to arrive; you must wait for imagery to give you realization. These insights will bring knowledge that is filled with power. That wisdom will connect you with your power, Bill.

I see something else in you as well, and this is a problem for you. You find a really potent subject and then wander away from the topic because you think you are finished with your insights. Then you try to fill in the gaps with superfluous information that has nothing to do with your genuine capacity to see, since complacency kicks in and you get bored. That's exactly what's happening now. You're trying to create subject matter, but you shouldn't try. If you try, you will never find the experience that you are waiting for. You must wait for it to come from within. Just like the next story you have for me.

Bill:

My concern at this point is that I have told you some of these stories in the past and you have never chosen to respond or speak to the power in them, if you did see any. I am afraid I will tell you and you will have no transmission or you won't see anything in the story.

Lujan:

Hold on. When we talked about these subjects a few years ago, I was trying to draw you away from those particular experiences because of your fixation upon the significance you had ascribed to them. Within that attachment you were holding onto an intellectual idea, a programmed response to your experience. It wasn't healthy.

The sorcery material that you were previously exposed to is embedded with multilayered information, which can easily introduce power plays into a warrior's psyche. There is so much room to dogmatically apply a kind of 'pseudo-warriorship' within the enigmatic premises outlined. This is very dangerous, as it can lead to getting lost in chasing shadows and entities. Warriors become programmed because the story appears to have no conclusion, via the fact that the full capacity to discover the insights eludes them, leaving no viable option to go beyond what has been outlined.

Your own story now loops in on itself, for you have become trapped in your own intellectualism. You are leaping to the next issue and the next subject, and you get frustrated because you don't feel like you are getting to the next level in your evolution as you think it should be happening. The fact is that you need to be waiting. Like most people in this day and age, you have forgotten how to wait for power. You are constantly grabbing for it. You must be patient, my friend.

THEY BITE

Bill:

Laying in my bed, my mind drifts to the one subject that I have pursued heavily for some years: Dreaming. I have become quite capable of entering into what is known as lucid dreaming, which is a technique of becoming conscious in your dreams. It took me several years of practice to get relatively proficient, following the methods discussed and taught in the works of a single author who published extensive material on this subject in the 1960s.

I started with the technique of finding my hands in my dreams. I moved on to being able to explore and change dream scenes as I chose. I often found myself wandering through odd and alien worlds as I changed from one scene to the next; from grey landscapes with no trees or shapes of any kind, to beautiful, rolling hills of grass with ice blue streams cutting across the landscape. Other times, I have walked black stone labyrinths that seemed to create a castle-like structure around me.

Whenever I shifted from a regular dream scene into lucid dreaming, I would always notice one unique trait: The story line of the dream I was in would instantly stop, and the people in the dream would vanish.

I have been walking down the street on my way to work, running late, when I would notice that I forgot to put on my pants and suddenly realize that I was in a dream. I would 'wake up', but still be on the street in the same scene; the difference being that, now, I didn't care that I didn't have pants on and the once busy street was now empty of its inhabitants.

I knew I was dreaming because I was free to go and do as I pleased with impunity. It didn't take me long to realize that, in this state, anyone that remained as a character in the dream scene was not an ordinary figment of my imagination. Most people that lingered seemed to be a conglomeration of alien energy. There have been many occasions in which I have actually been accosted by these beings in the dream realm.

In one such event, I found myself in an old world tavern. I had become aware that I was in an alternate realm and not an ordinary dream scene. I instantly grew nervous because of the fact that this tavern was still full of people. I had traveled within such realms long enough to know that these creatures should not be here, and yet they were. I became more than nervous when I realized there were about fifty of them in the room with me. As I mentioned before, when there are characters left in my dreaming scene they are not products of my own perception but energetic sources that command their own awareness.

The 'people' in the room didn't seem to have noticed me, and I meant to keep it that way. I imagined this must be what it felt like for a deep-sea diver to be surrounded by sharks that don't seem to detect or care about his presence – not yet anyway. I collected my thoughts for a moment and then did what any dream traveler would do when in an old world pub filled with alien sharks. I pulled up to the bar to get a drink. Why the hell not, right?

The bartender walked over to me and nodded as if to take my order. The second I spoke out loud – which is not something I did in dreaming as a rule – the entire congregation in the pub instantly became aware of my presence. They collectively pounced on me. It was almost as if they all knew I was there and were waiting for the trap to be sprung the moment I gave away the fact that I was not one of them. The fear of being trapped or pinned down in a world I didn't understand was beyond my imagination.

The swarm grabbed at me as if my very life force was something they could not live without. I screamed and shot upward like a rocket in an attempt to escape. With the sensation of flying through the many hands trying to hold me down, I awoke abruptly in my bed. The sheets were wet with sweat.

As if I hadn't learned my lesson already, I found myself, on another occasion, in a very different and odd dreamscape. This time I awoke suspended in the void itself. There was nothing but blackness all around, yet not a lack of light. I was capable of seeing myself, but there was nothing else to see. Within the first few seconds of my waking in this realm, I realized I was not alone. There were other things that seemed to be circling in the depths of the void that surrounded me.

Suddenly, I was grabbed by what seemed to be the darkness itself. There were three distinct entities. One had me by both ankles and one on either wrist. I was being stretched in the three different directions at once. I quickly began to fight back. My struggling caused me to start to swing like a pendulum, as if I were attached to some kind of invisible cord. I began to make huge arcs from apex to apex, all the while being chewed on by my dark assailants. I could clearly feel teeth biting into my ankles and wrists. The teeth of these creatures felt like long, tiny needles piercing my flesh. I fought harder and harder as I swung higher and faster through the void-like realm.

I can remember a wild emotion coming over me. I was afraid, but this time it was not the same terror I was accustomed to. This fear was exhilarating. I knew very well I was in a fight for my awareness, but I was thrilled with the battle. The rush was awesome and intense. I fought, but with a sense of detachment. I was alive with the combat and alive with the fear of it as well. The creatures seemed to be feeding on that very emotion, a feeling that I have never again felt.

Their teeth sunk deeper as I struggled to shed those ghastly beings. I can still remember the only glimpse I caught of my assailants. They were three heads and nothing more. Each head was jet black, but shadowy and dull. No eyes, just a head with a wide, leering mouth full of needle-like teeth. With one last thrash, I was able to free myself from that realm.

The second I found myself in my bed again, I became acutely aware of the sensation of a claw-like hand still on my left ankle. The feeling was so real that I had to pull back the sheet to make sure there wasn't something really there. I had the strangest feeling something had come back across with me.

Did I bring something back with me from the dream realm? Is that even possible?

Lujan:

Yes, it is possible, and you may very well have. The shaman and sorcerers whose stories have become the most widely known seem to have indicated that one must go into dreaming to forge the energy body. The main author who has written about this subject discussed only four gates of dreaming, but mentioned seven without going into further detail. I can confirm that there are eight gates. Perhaps this individual did not have the knowledge of all the other gates. Whether he did or not, it is dangerous to only discuss partial information like that. People have been brought to a certain threshold but cannot discover what's on the next level, for they have been left with no further guidance.

The reason that we are here on this planet as human beings is to fortify our energetic existence. Even though we manifest organically, in reality we are all inorganic by nature. We all exude light, yet we perceive that we are denser than that as we are confronted with the inevitability of our physical form and therefore believe we are going to die, and then we do. All things in this universe that are organically based are faced with this. The universe itself is breaking down, and we are a representation of our current understanding of that process, until our collective belief systems evolve beyond this limited premise. Since there is an end to our physical existence, we are thus alerted to the fact that we must come into contact with our true holographic self while we're here.

Although there is a lot of shamanic material indicating that one must go into dreaming to forge the Double, or the energetic self, this is totally misleading. Teaching seers to forge their photonic potential in a realm that is removed from our organic existence – within dreaming – is truly dangerous. In doing this you relocate your energetic being into facets of reality that are completely beyond your control. So you make yourself vulnerable to portions of your energy being pecked at, all throughout your dreaming experiences, by those ancient awarenesses that observe and track us when we appear in their domain.

By merely venturing into those realms, you leave your energetic footprint in areas you will never visit again. Through the fact that you were there, you deposit a portion of your memory. And if your curiosity or desire for more is hooked, you will try to pursue this through your waking life, attempting to return over and over to replicate what you have done before.

There is a very ancient technique involving the photonic eye, which is the third eye viewing capacity that sees within dimension. This is known nowadays as 'remote viewing', and is when a seer projects and relocates their seeing somewhere else within the first attention. That is, to a place within this reality that does actually exist.

The seer can view the location, and the person or actions taking place within that space and time. This energetic relocation of perception is exactly what you are doing in dreaming. The difference is that in this world when you come back to where you are physically stationed, your photonic potential returns to your body and you become energetically whole again.

In dreaming, as I said, a piece of energy is left behind and absorbed by that realm visited. The entities that drew you to that region will utilize that energy to visually manifest themselves, and an image of you, simultaneously, in correspondence with what you expect to see. Manifestation takes energy and in this case it's your energy. The question is: Where have you left it? In another realm that you could neither understand nor have any real control over.

Bill:

Is this how I brought something across the dreaming divide? Did that entity use my energy as a bridge of sorts?

Lujan:

Yes, but that is not even the true consequence of the situation. The real problem is that you now have something constantly utilizing your life force, your photonic energy. Imagine that times a thousand, or however many times you go into dreaming! By pursuing this activity you become infused with immense amounts of that foreign energy, with your essence dispersed in far-removed positions that you will have no means of returning to. Then your energy is being siphoned and this becomes a multiplex of utilization of your energy body. By allowing your photonic eye to leave your organic body like this, you become accessible to all kinds of alien awareness and, as a result, your intelligence becomes something alien in itself.

Bill:

Let me see if I have this. When we go into dreaming, we are traveling into other realms and leaving a piece of our energy and our awareness, and the intelligence there consumes and suckles on our life force like a piglet to a mother hog?

Lujan:

Not exactly. Here is where you have to get away from your paranoia. If you decide to pursue second attention fixations, you make yourself vulnerable to inorganic influence. The awareness there does not suck on your life force; it utilizes it, meaning it blends with it and this becomes a joining of you and them. You will absorb part of this entity and it will absorb part of you.

Bill:

So every time you go there, you blend with something in that realm?

Lujan:

Right. Some people say that this process is stabilizing that dreaming position in order to have the possibility to return; however, this is simply not true. There will be hundreds of thousands of positions that you will neither be able to utilize, nor ever really be able to return to. Although it may appear that one is accessing a previously visited site, this is an illusion.

Our energy is meant to be gathered in the central matrix of our human essence, which is our heart. This then beckons our true energetic counterpart, the Double, to integrate within the reality of the world we live in, by virtue of the fact that our electromagnetic potency activates our third eye capacity. On the other hand, if we become caught within second attention pursuits, then all our precious energy that feeds our third eye resource will mingle with what we encounter and be dramatically diminished through that absorption.

Bill:

Wow! This is startling. I didn't quite finish telling you the entire story. It didn't take long for me to realize that I had indeed brought something back from that dreamscape with me. Within a few weeks of that dream, I sensed something living in the house with my wife and me.

I noticed what I started to call a 'pesky shadow' - an entity that looked like a small, fast-moving, dark blur. I would see it dart under doors and around corners, but would usually catch only a glimpse of it out of the corner of my eye. I decided to ignore this thing, which did not go over well, because it only increased its efforts to bother me. I knew I was not imagining it because my wife saw it, too. I had never mentioned it to her for I figured she would blame me for it being in the house, which she did.

One time, when I was away traveling and she was home alone with our dog, I got a frantic call in the night from her. She was very upset. She said that she was sleeping when someone came to our door and started ringing the bell repeatedly. The dog flew out of the room, barking and growling. She went to investigate, wielding a frying pan, ready to do battle with whatever person who thought waking her up like that was funny. She threw open the door, only to find there was nobody there. She assumed it was kids ringing the bell and running away, but since she was awake now I might as well be too, so she called.

When I was done laughing, she was not in any better a mood. She demanded, "What the hell is so funny about kids waking me up in the middle of the night like that?" and I said, "Honey, we don't have a doorbell!"

This 'pesky shadow' was quite capable of creating a variety of audible illusions, from the non-existent doorbell ringing to whispering in my ear when I was sleeping. I quickly got tired of being woken up to, "Hey... Hey... Hey," in my left ear.

A few months after this event, I was having a party at my home. I have a staircase that leads to the upstairs part of the house, which is dark and rarely used. A female friend of mine had excused herself to the bathroom. Myself and the rest of the congregation were in the living room. Suddenly, she came scooting back into the party with a most strange look on her face.

I caught a cutting glance from my wife. I already knew what was up, but I walked over to my friend anyway to see.

"Everything okay?" I asked.

With a slightly embarrassed look on her face, she answered yes. I said that I didn't believe her, and she then told me that as she was coming out of the bathroom, the darkness in the hall had lunged out at her, as if to grab her as she passed by.

"Really? You don't say!" I replied in my most serious voice, and handed her another drink.

Lujan:

(Giggling at me.) Now, since you unwittingly drew that entity into your home that's ringing your phantom doorbell, what it's doing is absorbing the energy that you would use to perceive your own Double. By occupying you within the machinations of its mischievous character, not only is it utilizing your precious photonic potential, it's draining the power within your environment through harassing you to capture your attention.

Ultimately what needs to happen is for you to wait patiently for your Double to reveal itself to you through your own acts of responsibility, power, and integrity in your life. Now, when I speak of the Double, you must understand that I am not referring to the concept of a second self that is forged in dream realms. This idea is erroneous. The energy Double, by virtue of you being here, is on this planet with you. You just don't yet have the energy to see it or to draw it to you. This is partly due to the fact that you have used your photonic potential in superfluous activities in dreaming and the waking world.

The Double will dream this world into realities beyond measure, beyond anything you could ever imagine. Its arrival represents a multidimensional integration with our unencumbered human potential. Most seers who become aware of this choose not to have anything to do with second attention fixations. They know for a fact that this pursuit drains their potential into unmanageable activities. Unfortunately, countless seers have been lost within their desire to traverse the second attention as a facet of their wish to be enlightened. These individuals absorb and employ methods on those dreaming journeys that draw others into webs of indirect involvement, and this actually corrodes their personal power and neutralizes their ability to see clearly.

This photonic drain and consequent subterfuge occur due to the surplus of energy it takes to focus on and maintain these other realities that cater to our awareness. Second attention inorganic beings adapt to our awareness through coupling with our photonic potential, since it is composed of the energy that sustains them. When dreaming, we are unwittingly engaged in this way and thus we blend with worlds that are intrinsically selfish and consuming. As we merge with this intention we then become selfish and consuming ourselves. We mistakenly assume that these realities have power.

That ongoing loss of vital energy is like a bathtub with a faucet leaking into it. It will drip for days and then, after a period of time, we notice that the tub is full. Those single drops end up becoming a huge mass of investment in something that you didn't know was happening. All of a sudden you realize that your energy has been utilized in unforeseen areas. Your life as a seer has been waylaid, and at the end of your journey you may not have the resources to cross over to where you are meant to arrive. All of your vital energy has been invested in constructs that have no relevance in comparison to the power available to you in this world, where your true heart path awaits. Do you understand this, Bill?

Bill:

It seems that we should not go out into the universe, scattering our energy in other realms through dreaming. We need to be gathering our energy here in our centralized matrix, our own body, to bring the Double here to us.

Lujan:

Well, like I said, it is erroneous to imagine that the Double is anywhere else but here. It is interdimensionalized within the human domain but momentarily veiled by a very subtle frequency, which we cannot pierce while we are enthralled, whether that be within the intricacies of the second attention or the dramas of the waking world. We can only wait patiently for the Double to come into close proximity, via our acts of integrity and power.

The catch is, Bill, that you will not know that you have collected enough gravity to draw it towards yourself until it happens, so you must be of service to your environment and know what you are waiting for, even though you are not waiting. To become aware of the consequences of gestures in general, you have to cultivate enough intelligence in the waking world to realize where your energies are being unnecessarily utilized and where you are being waylaid.

Remember, this world is a mirror of what's happening in the other attention, and vice versa. We must wake up to what's really occurring. We have to bring our full power into our waking reality and not focus on an alternate holographic construct that has coercively manipulated our consciousness. The destruction of our planet right in front of our very eyes is a clear indication that we are not living the way we are supposed to as a species. This is an obvious reflection of the inorganic influence upon our waking reality. If we can be manipulated there, we can be manipulated here, via the Machiavellian methods that run permeate humanity as a result of this interference.

CROSSING OVER

Bill:

You said that we 'cross over' at the moment of our death. Where is it that we are crossing over to?

Lujan:

That will be revealed at the moment of our death. You cannot define what your death is going to give you. Your death will reveal where you will arrive when it happens. As far as I know, very few people have any control over this factor. I have been shown exactly where I am going, but I have no influence over the outcome. My situation is unusual in that I know where the gateway to my inevitable end is and what the feeling will be when I arrive, but I have no idea what is going to present itself to me after the fact.

The doors that open up one's perception to our inevitability are usually heavily veiled, thus disallowing full awareness upon the point of one's departure. It is virtually impossible for most people in the evolutionary phase we are in to say, "I am deciding how I am going to die, and when, and exactly what that process will contain." This very agenda is just like when someone comes along and demands to be validated, or to be given what they expect, to bolster their idea of themselves.

When I am faced with this solicitation as a Nagual, I am obligated to communicate what is necessitated through the intervention of Spirit. In receiving this gesture from the unknown, the individual will be presented with the same factor that they will be faced with at their death. The truth is that we will all be met with what we need, not what we want.

It is imperative that we as human beings stand resolute and apply ourselves in the moment with the power that we contain from within. Nevertheless, there will be moments that will create regret, regardless of the power that flowed through us at the point that we arrived upon, for the social eddy is continually attempting to insert itself so as to derail the seer's perspective. Dealing with that regret and choosing how to apply oneself is where wisdom is truly reflected back to the warrior's path, when we put into practice what we have learnt. We have to face the consequences of our energetic outlay, and we cannot really know what the full implications of our actions, collectively and individually, will be.

It all comes down to the individual in the end, but nobody's perfect and everyone is accountable. You and I are accountable right now. If we diverge from what is essential, our inevitability will bear witness. And if we don't take responsibility for our life we will lose our very precious connection with the unknown factor. When we traverse incorrectly and refuse to take note of what presents itself, our life becomes wretched. Within this desperation it is very difficult to see the subtle nuances that are the communications of our heart path, beckoning us home.

To reiterate, if we lose access to this magical facility of reception through acts of denial, then it becomes very difficult to get back to the seat of our power. To retrieve the truth of that which was set forth as an illusion is extremely complex, as this process provokes the catharsis of coming face to face with the fact that you haven't been real. This process may transform into a time of sorrow, which is where great wisdom is obtained. However, those periods of deep transformation will not be reached if one is extensively engaged with inorganic beings, for they will endeavor to prevent the self-reflective process from occurring.

As I have already explained, by going into the dreaming world of an entity, you expose yourself to extensive manipulation. Such entities can then take a portion of your energy and use it to manifest themselves in this reality, even if it is just as a shadow that once lurched out of the darkness, or as the creature that is stalking you at this very moment. That entity is trying to make you realize something and we have to get to the bottom of what that is.

Bill:

Okay, so, at the moment, if I have made those mistakes in the past by going into dreaming and that entity has borrowed some of my energy and--

Lujan:

(Cutting me off in mid sentence:) No! You can't say that you have made that mistake. You can say that you are living the consequences of your actions in this moment. That is never a mistake. What is hazardous is to live recklessly. What you are endeavoring to do now is live your life with sobriety, to implement your energy in the world correctly, since you are attempting to take into full consideration what you have learnt. You are claiming responsibility for your choices from now on, because you can't change what you've done. You cannot live a mistake right now; you can only live the reality that is presenting itself to you in this moment. And that means you have to live with integrity, and if you do, your acts will be acts of power, regardless of what you think has been a misapplication.

Bill:

I guess what I am trying to ask is this: Is there a way to recover that lost energy from those realms?

Lujan:

Yes, by living in a state of power, by not regretting your actions and by remolding your perceptions in correspondence with the insight that comes upon you. You can apply this in all situations, including through your interaction with the entity that has integrated itself within your life. Even if it's annoying the hell out of you right now, you have to live in the reality that you have created and take responsibility for it as best you can. That is when your life becomes an act of power. That circumstance will wrestle with you in an attempt to teach you to become fully detached from the drama that has enthralled you.

Bill:

Yeah, it's certainly doing that.

Lujan:

This will give you the ability to see the intricate labyrinth that has been staged by its presence and has possessed your attention through its base enactments. This is where your non-involvement will become your ultimate ally, by virtue of the fact that your clear awareness will change the circumstance. Now we have returned full circle to the original sorcery teachings, but with a new understanding of the old way.

Bill:

Let me see if I understand something you said earlier when you spoke about crossing over. It seems to me that this is a consequence of our ability to store energy in our lives. If we store enough energy, we cross over at the moment of our death; if not, we don't?

Lujan:

Tell me one person who has saved up enough energy to live forever. No one. No matter how much energy you accumulate you cannot avoid your inevitable end. You can utilize your experiences to implement your wisdom in your environment, and that will have an energetic impact. But there are no surpluses to be had; everyone dies.

Bill:

I am not suggesting living forever, but there seems to be a threshold that you do or don't cross depending on the integrity of your life and an energetic accumulation of that path traveled.

Lujan:

You utilize your energy. I know irrefutably that somebody like a very old Native on a reservation in the Americas, who has very little time left but has accumulated deep insights, will have the capacity to transmit, even though they are on the verge of their inevitable end. By virtue of the fact that they have applied themselves wholeheartedly to their world, their perception will enable them to reapply its wisdom to their environment so they can reflect this back to their community as insight. They won't live forever, but their input will continue as long as it is absorbed. When this insight is filtered back, the collective consciousness will inevitably expand and blossom. It's very important to keep a finger on this pulse, or we have people and society going back to square one.

CONTINUUM: ENCOUNTERS AND ORIGINS

Bill:

I have been wondering about your benefactors. Where were they? You discussed going into the Dream Maker's Realm in one of your previous books to be instructed by them. Did they go there at the time of their death? Did you meet these people in their waking life? Were they alive from a physical perspective when you met them in that realm?

(Lujan describes how he met his benefactors and received shamanic transmission in an alternate reality in his first book, 'The Art of Stalking Parallel Perception'.)

Lujan:

This is an extremely complex question to answer. I was subject to the reflection of their wisdom, to the manifestation of their intention and their ability to be there for me. This is transdimensional interactivity; it is so intertwining within its intricacy. For example, I have actually seen within another person his connectivity to an alternate self, a Hopi Indian fire-gazer shaman who is still living five hundred years ago.

He presented himself as a conscious presence through the arrival of his attention. He showed me where he was by gazing through my student's eyes at me from an incomprehensible distance. This shaman knows that if he deems it necessary to make a quantum leap, he can transport himself through the container that is my student, awaiting his arrival. Both are subtly aware of each other, yet my student had to be reminded, and still to this day doesn't know exactly what he is waiting for. Yet he pines for a part of himself that eternally calls his awareness to awaken.

I know this is hard to understand. The sequence of that ancient shaman's time continuum still exists, while simultaneously an alignment, in terms of a transdimensional leap, is possible via the fact that my student's time continuum is available to him through the universal predetermination that is their symbiotic third eye process. In essence, because of this connection, they are one being separated by time and space.

As you can see, this introduces multiple ramifications in terms of our concurrent existences as human beings. The attention of this shaman connects through resonance, which creates the feeling of longing within my student. This is the only way for a transdimensional leap to occur, to know the origin and feel the destination. All that is of consequence within their respective experiences will become part of their mutual consciousness, initiating the etheric alignment that will necessitate the gravity to allow that quantum integration to occur. For instance in this case, my student has to gather the essential power to enable his Double to come close to him so that the fire-gazer can make this leap.

Such possibilities are open to everybody. We are dimensionalized to such a degree that this so-called solid reality that we currently inhabit, and the linear fixation by which we understand it, don't really exist. We know everyone dies, yet there is a process whereby nothing is dying. We continually thrive; but can we remember the complex facets of that eternal existence to aid us on our journey as human beings?

Every reality that ends is also a beginning and yet, the beginning never really happened. These parallel continuums, which are compartmentalized into different times and spaces, are actually unified. They exist as one. So the timeline that unfolds from a linear perspective, of me being a child and being taken by my benefactor, the old Nagual Lujan, was part of his reality despite centuries having passed. He stepped through time and space to intervene in the early years of my life, hundreds of years later from a chronological perspective. This is similar to the way that old Native shaman peered from his time continuum into mine, through the eyes of my student.

Bill:

What was the result of seeing these old shamans?

Lujan:

The result of interacting with my benefactors was reflections of insights. Insights that shaped me as a human being and are shaping you now, Bill. Our experiences always change us.

DREAMS AND VISIONS

Bill:

You tell me that you don't have any dreams of any kind, only visions. Could you tell me more about the difference between regular dreaming and lucid dreaming, as far as the energetic consequence of encountering entities and so forth?

Lujan:

Normal or random dreaming is completely different from dream visions. In most cases, what one encounters in the second attention are just incoherent projections borne of unresolved feelings from one's waking life. You will not come in contact with entities on those occasions; you will only meet yourself. Remember, even people that say they practice lucid dreaming are still governed by the innate proclivities that belong to their character. If you are not resolved in life, you will not be resolved in your lucid dreams or your regular dreams. If people are jerks in their waking world, they're still jerks in their dreams!

(Lujan is laughing with abandon.)

In ordinary dreaming you are just living out the bent of your character in a realm that will cater to you, because it *is* you, magnified. How can you escape from yourself, let alone something else covertly placed? When we are sitting here in this reality, it is a holographic universe that is a perfect projection of how we've organized it. Can I step out of it at will? Not really. I know the nexus of it; I know where I am empty, but for the time I am meant to be here, I am here.

When I go off in visions, my body is still here. We have to deal with this reality, take the fables and illusions away from people. This is a serious business, living, as we're dying, but that doesn't mean we can't enjoy it.

Bill:

The most popular teachings on sorcery advise going into dreaming to gather that alien energy and add it to your own. They indicate that you need that energy to progress to the next level of your shamanic journey. Why do they think that energetically blending with those dreaming entities is a good thing?

Lujan:

The three-pronged Nagual who transmitted this information had been prompted to go into dreaming by his teacher. His general characteristics were seen as a dictum of Spirit indicating that this path must be taken. That guidance was not destined to emphasize this way for others but was prescribed for him alone. Many elders, including those of the Huichol people, believe that it is not their right to advise an initiate not to undertake a path that may be detrimental. They would not wish to interfere with what would ultimately transpire, thus revealing who the person really is. Whether the apprentice's personal traits are seen as black or white, in terms of the magic they arrive upon, all initiate Naguals that are instructed within the first attention are watched very carefully, in terms of their personal proclivities, so as to discern a healer from a brujo.

In my case, I was taught directly within the second attention, so I was not subject to this approach. Within my apprenticeship, which in actuality was a transmission of consciousness, I was instructed as to the implications of second attention fixations. So I was not influenced by the aggressive nature of the inorganics' ability to coercively maneuver consciousness away from one's essential truths.

Let me ask you, Bill, getting back to the subject at hand: Would you want to go into a hostile territory and fight with someone predatorial that wants to kill you, and has the capability to do so, just so you can retrieve some of their energy, then return and openly declare, "I've acquired dark powers. Anybody want to mess with me?"

No one in their right mind would want anything to do with you. Everybody knows that you can't resonate with a higher frequency by taking on a low frequency potential.

"I've absorbed this sinister resonance, want to see it?"

How does that even sound to you?

"I went into an inorganic realm of the universe and did battle with a demon that wanted to steal my soul, but instead I stole a portion of its essence by stalking it and then quickly escaping its grasp when it attempted to fully blend with my life force. I'm now going to use this dark energy to forward my enlightenment."

Honestly, what the hell is that? It's ridiculous.

(*Lujan's infectious laughter disarms my seriousness as usual.*)

Bill:

Okay, you make a profound point here. I just wondered why the Nagual in those books would tell his apprentice to go into those realms to gather that energy.

Lujan:

The only thing I will say is that the Nagual knew his student had no self-control, so he advised him to go into dreaming to gather and subdue the essential essence of an inorganic being's life force and attempt to bring that photonic potential back. In reality this was intended to show him the ultimate futility of either attempting to take or subdue another's potential, from a true evolutionary perspective. Obviously this lesson was not entirely absorbed. However, the Nagual had no choice but to follow the dictums of Spirit within that circumstance.

It was neither his fault nor the fault of the student that this information has been transmitted to the masses as a prescription for the warrior's way. Unfortunately, many have followed this formula as a tool to apply to their own lives, and have attempted to live vicariously through these tales of power. These accounts in actuality describe the gentle observance of the teacher, peering into an alternate reality that was his apprentice's personal journey.

The Nagual knew that no good would come of his student's inorganic interactions, yet could not stop him proceeding down a road that is irreversible once delved into too deeply. So, while he was under his tutelage, the Nagual had to observe what would arrive upon the path of his initiate and was always communicating to him: You don't need to be possessively connected to anything. You have everything you need right in front of you.

The directives of Juan Matus' lineage were not to indulge in the ways of the old sorcerers, but to pursue freedom within the human domain, a path with heart. We are inorganically bound; this is irrefutable, yet we are organically based. Our future as seers will be determined through reclaiming our independence, our sovereign right to be dimensionalized.

Bill:

Sounds like what you have been teaching me all along. Through taking responsibility in our lives, we can gather all the power and energy we need. This is our light energy.

Lujan:

Right. And this can be applied in your everyday life. In observing powerful human beings who have made a tremendous impact, such as Martin Luther King or Mahatma Gandhi or Mother Theresa, we can see that they were essentially good people with enormous amounts of insight, who applied their energy unflinchingly. They delved into themselves and helped humanity rise above their burdens. Being of service goes beyond the selfish desire to gain power.

The key to one's true nature is revealed in one's character. There is too often something covert embedded within, which is a wish to gain the upper hand. Through procedurally applying themselves to their circumstance, people try to obtain what is not theirs. Even though this idea of gaining control over others is an illusion, it is a serious one at that. The predator within wants to possess our potential, to cloak the innocence of light beings and steer them off their path by manipulating their awareness. Applying ourselves in this way towards each other amounts to replicating exactly the same behavior that has been pressed upon us for millennia.

That is how the predatorial influence operates; by tricking you, adding itself to you and whispering what you want to hear, without revealing what you really need to know, all the while supplying the idea that you are the source of the distortions that are being fed into your consciousness.

The installed voice mimics a magical faculty that all human beings possess, which resides in a very deep, subtle state of silent consciousness. The pseudo version of this, which is known as the dreaming emissary, is an inorganic, behind-the-scenes director, even though it openly interacts with you auditorially. It will only inform you of what you already know, but in a way that makes it seem like you discovered it, so that you will bask in the glow of your own brilliance as you reflect upon that incestuous communication. These are not your true insights or realizations but instead are hinge points to lever your pride and vanity. Inorganic predators know of this doorway and enter unabashedly behind your back.

Bill:

I have encountered this phenomenon and, now that I think about it, it did fit the description that you give.

Lujan:

When we talk you say, "I understand," or, "I have been doing that." All you need is a little prod to access exactly what you know, without me tricking or bargaining with you. You just get it when I speak about it. That's not how these emissaries work. They will inform you in a way to keep themselves in a position to bargain for your attention by saying, "Do you want to know something else? I will tell you whatever you want to know." They will cater to your every whim. That doesn't sound like a good thing to me.

Let's say you're dreaming in a separate reality, or you are just falling asleep, and a voice speaks to you. Isn't the universe a mirror? It tells you what you already know while you are in an altered state and you can't quite remember it. It seems like a revelation, but the truth is that when you went into that subtle shift of consciousness and got some insight into what you wanted to understand, that knowledge was already residing dormant within you. Unknown to you, you had already been applying this knowing to your life, though you were not yet totally conscious of what you were doing.

Mimicry and retranslation is the way these emissaries operate. Their voices are nothing but the extension of human machinations, reflecting back to us what we already are. And if that's what you are, then what is going to grab you by the ankles are sharp teeth and the fear of the consequences of being in contact with the violence that you have embedded in yourself. Do you hear me, Bill?

Bill:

You're describing me.

Lujan:

That's right. That's why I am talking to you about this. So when you come to terms with who you are and what your capabilities are, your true characteristics will become an enhancement, not a detriment. You feel this way because you are not truly proud of who you are, so you bring back all these horrendous things with you. You need to come to terms with these personal factors, for at the moment you do not have control over those tendencies and you would like to be something more.

All you have to do is say, "That's my power. That's my ability to run like an elk and not trip over." But when the elk gets teeth, you forget yourself and you get caught up in the passion of the fight. Stop that, and then you won't have to get worried about people seeing your naked butt in dreams! (*Both of us are howling with laughter now.*)

ENERGETIC ANCHORING

Bill:

I have some more questions about the three entities that attacked me in dreaming. When I was grabbed by the limbs, they were trying to blend with my energy, weren't they?

Lujan:

Perhaps, perhaps not. I have had a similar experience, linked to a student I was treating with shamanic healing who had three inorganics around him. How strange that you also have three entities around you. These beings became alerted to the fact that I was aware of them. I told my student that I had seen the entities around him and that they were passing through my body as I worked on him. A few days later, they came to me while I was sleeping and tried to drag down and pin my photonic energy under my house as I slept.

If a sorcerer wants to subdue another seer's power and stop their seeing, they will seek to bring their energy down. I have had a dark magician attempt to do this to me, when I lived in Bali, by obtaining the blood of a dead man and putting it at the top of the doorframe leading into my house. The idea is that the blood will attempt to return to the ground, since the man has already been buried, and when you pass under it, the consequences are that it will draw your energy down with it. A dark sorcerer would apply that kind of energetic anchoring to trap you in realms governed by the same kind of beings that tried to drag you down in dreaming.

Although this was a separate instance from dealing with the entities around my student, the basic maneuver was the same. In both cases, there was an attempt to pin my energy to the ground. This illustrates a basic law of the universe. If you want to subdue a light being, you take them down or energetically bury them, so to speak. This is very much like when a warrior is fighting and falls; something is depleted if their body hits the ground. We can observe this as a fundamental rule. We have to endeavor to stay energetically upright, to remain standing.

Bill:

How literal are you being here? What if we sit or lay on the ground?

Lujan:

Of course you can sit or lay on the ground. Your destiny will determine your ultimate inevitability in each circumstance, regardless of where you place yourself.

Bill:

What happened to you and the sorcerer in Bali? What did you do about him putting blood above your door? How did you even know that he did that in the first place?

Lujan:

The first thing I did was to burn a bundle of incense sticks. I washed the walls and doors with smoke to see if he had done anything to the house. I suspected this person might try something like this, as he didn't like me too much. He was jealous and unsure of how to handle my presence in his territory, if you will.

As soon as I put the smoking incense under the affected doorframe, the sticks burst into open flame. I knew then some kind of witchcraft had been applied but I was not versed in Balinese magic, so I asked a local friend of mine about it. He was a good man who knew of the dark magic in the area and told me what the other had likely done. He also said that this particular shaman was known for subduing the life force and energy of others.

Placing blood above a door is used to lower one's heart frequency, due to the symbiotic communication that takes place between all blood, thereby undermining the energetic stability of those who walk underneath it. This will allow a sorcerer to further anchor your energy to the ground and subdue you with dark practices, whether they are socially or supernaturally applied.

As a buoyant light being, you would be operating at too high of an energetic potential to be taken down all at once without first being weakened. An adversary must diminish your light frequency so that people will reflect on you differently. Then he can manipulate their idea of you, for when your life energy is reduced you become tired and you don't make your associates feel good when they're around you any more. Here is where a dark sorcerer will come in and tip the scales by degrading your status within the eyes of those around you, pushing you out of their social circle, thus further isolating you into the 'us and them' factor. That's black magic.

Bill:

It all seems pretty evil and complicated.

Lujan:

It is. And I will also tell you that there are people in the world who are very talented in tantric and Asian magic, whose resourcefulness goes beyond what you would imagine. Some of them are extremely powerful and have a bent of nature that can produce an active reflection of themselves in other realities.

Bill:

So that means those entities that attacked me could have been reflections of sorcerers that live or lived in the world?

Lujan:

That, or they could be genuine entities. You will never know. For myself, I have no desire to go to realms like that to find out whether such apparitions are a product of human attention or of alien awareness. I don't want any part of it. If you have clean feet, why go out of your way to step in mud?

Bill:

I have to admit this is a little unsettling. What should the average person or a burgeoning seer do to protect themselves from such an assault, from someone more powerful and with an energetically predatory nature? In 'The Art of Stalking Parallel Perception' you discuss an attack from a shaman of a similar description. The man knew of your gathering strength and wanted to halt your progress as a seer. So he sent a shadow entity to intercept you, which appeared as a grey whirlwind at the foot of your bed. What should I do if I find myself in a similar situation?

Lujan:

All you can do is collect your energy and love your life and those around you. If you encounter people that won't let you love them, then be very careful. You will feel a sense of distortion when you are around those individuals. They are twisted inside, and they will want you to be twisted too, so that you will be like them. If you're not like them, then your clarity will intimidate them and that's when they can become dangerous. Be kind to such people, but limit your interaction with them.

This is the reality we live within. You can't always decide who you are around, such as coworkers or other people in your environment that you can't avoid. You will have no power over them or their actions, so the only thing you can do is to be responsible for yourself when you are near them. You do this by being careful with your input and mindful of how you interact.

Know who you are dealing with. Don't poke the beehive. They will furiously fly all around and act like they are going to sting you, but you must remember that they are not you. Remain calm and eventually they will settle down and leave you alone when they realize you are not a threat.

For example, I was doing my morning workout the other day and I noticed a hornets' nest near my exercise equipment. I don't particularly like hornets and I was faced with a decision at this point. Do I swat down the nest and run back in the house screaming like a banshee, or do I trust that these beings will know that I won't hurt them and we will coexist peacefully? I have not harmed their nest and they have not stung me either. Yet in the same breath, if there were a big black widow spider on my equipment I would not put my hand on it. There are certain things you just don't do.

Bill:

Okay. You said you wouldn't touch a dangerous spider if it were in your immediate area, but what if the dark shaman was this spider that has come too close to you? What do you do if you are under attack or in a situation like this?

Lujan:

The magic here is to live your life with such harmony that the wasps, spiders, and dark sorcerers don't actually focus on you.

Bill:

That's nice, but sometimes battle is inevitable. Sometimes the spider is there or the wolf is at the door. Then what?

Lujan:

(Laughing) I don't know. Sometimes you do have to kill the spider. Sometimes you do have to remove something from your environment or a battle is inevitable, but you can't preempt those situations. You can't have a plan on how to conduct a battle that isn't facing you at this point. You have to wait until you are in that situation and then do whatever you have to do to solve the problem. You can't know what you are going to do until you do it. All you can have as weapons for that battle are your innocence and your integrity. Anything more than that is black magic. And even uprightness can be bent into righteous indignation, which can be perceived as white magic; but that's not right either. It is still interference.

Bill:

Sounds like neither is good.

Lujan:

That's right, neither is good. Both focus on an outcome that may never manifest, or a result that you are trying to bring about. Both are a waste of energy, both are futile. No matter what you do, inevitability faces you at the moment you have to act. That's using your death as an advisor. You can't say, "Come on death, come and advise me. Tell me what I should do in this situation."

You have to wait until the tiger pounces to be able to truly know what you are going to do. You don't go and poke a tiger with a stick to use your death as an advisor. That would be complete nonsense.

As funny as this may be, it's truly a shame that people adopt this kind of approach, for this distorts their perception into thinking that they have some sort of control over their inevitability. We do not.

What is inevitable will be past at the moment that you realize it, and that is all we have. What's important is that, as that passing moment goes by, you may remember something that previously impacted you. Here you are using your death as an advisor, for that memory affirms that you had the necessary power to retrieve something that is a valuable piece of the puzzle, or wisdom that makes you a stronger warrior.

A strong warrior does not go poking tigers, but waits for the message of the past to come back and advise them on how to act upon the future. It usually happens retrospectively. Inevitability is a strange facet of a warrior's life. Death is always coming up from behind. Inevitability is nothing to be played with.

RESONANCE

Bill:

I have a question about something that has been on my mind lately. Are all the realms outside of this one aggressive or evil? It seems that everywhere but here is dark and menacing. Is there no other realm of light beings, like we humans?

Lujan:

It's not really a good idea to dwell upon the negative, Bill, by virtue of the fact that it will bring that resonance to you. You must be aware of the dangers around you, but be unattached, simultaneously. There are things that you have to avoid, but if you are in a state of consciousness that is truly progressive for a light being, then you won't indulge in that preoccupation. Those realms won't exist for you, for their influence won't penetrate. It's when you take on the idea that there is good and evil that you become pitted against yourself in terms of black and white.

Bill:

I don't understand you.

Lujan:

I know you don't, because you are so used to the dualistic factor within your social interpretations. If there is a dualistic basis, then there is going to be good and there is going to be evil. There is going to be something terribly frightful and adversarial to deal with. We need to move our consciousness away from this dualism and see everything as a pure reflection of ourselves, from a holographic perspective.

There are a lot of seemingly contradictory elements that reveal themselves and we just have to come to terms with this until we begin to truly see the complex labyrinth that extends beyond the reasonable assessments of the mind. Remember, it's not my belief system I am describing but the interdimensional virtual reality in which we live. This is an interesting phrase, since 'virtual' is holographic, and reality is a projection of our consciousness as a group.

Every single thing you see carries virtually the same DNA that is inside of you. We commune, affecting each other's biological structure, which brings about our perception. Although it seems that the holographic universe that we view in the first attention remains static, apart from the wind blowing the leaves on a tree or rocks falling down a hill, in actual fact an enormous exchange is occurring in every single moment. It's so very complex yet simple in the same breath.

This is a terribly difficult journey. Everybody has to go through it. You have to be there with yourself. There is nobody here to protect us but our self. And if everything becomes us, then we know the journey that we're on is just a reflection of who we are. You don't understand me, do you?

Bill:

Not at all.

Lujan:

Well, at least you are listening. You are showing the same amount of interest in this as you would show in something that occupies you in an obsessive way, because you are fascinated by danger. If you want danger, it will find you.

Bill:

No shit! I have figured that out.

Lujan:

Yes. But even if you are not interested in danger, it comes for you anyway. You have to realize that you must be humble enough to see it coming and try to get out of the way. If you can't manage to do that in time, your fate confronts you with that adversity. This is unfortunate but it is the reality we are living in. We have to learn to cope with this dualistic factor with a unifying view.

You need to endeavor to be totally impartial within your neutrality. Even if your body is screaming from inside because you know everything outside you is desperately trying to recalibrate your energy field, you have to stay steadfast. Eventually your detached adaptations will become your ability to help those without power to transcend the reality of violence and pain that they project outwardly.

REMOTE VIEWING, DREAMING AND THE PHOTONIC EYE

Bill:

When in dreaming, the sensation that we are somehow participating in creating the reality that surrounds us is quite pronounced at times. If this kind of interactivity is happening in the waking world, how can we start to become aware of it?

Lujan:

It is at once incredibly intricate, yet so very simple. When you drop a pebble in the middle of a pond, the concentric ripples affect the whole body of water. Even from a linear perspective, when you are observing the act itself you become caught in the visual anomaly which is the wave that is a minute tsunami making its way to the shore, and then upon its arrival, returning to its source. As you know, the first wave is stronger than the ripple that returns, and this within itself is absolutely indicative of our consciousness.

For us to arrive upon anything other than what is obvious, we must patiently bear witness to our ever-present reality subtly converging in on itself, delivering us to nuances that we would never have expected to find. This is our journey; what we absorb just depends on whether we take notice of what's really going on or not. In other words, it's not the initial act that matters; it's the consequence of our observance that allows us to grow.

Let me give you another kind of example that has to do with the outcomes of observations. There have been studies done over the years where people have demonstrated remote viewing. The test subject is put into a room and some distance away, in another room, a randomly selected playing card is placed face down on a table. The test subject is asked to 'view' the card. Keep in mind that there is no way the subject could physically see or know beforehand which card it is.

The aim of this experiment is to get these people to focus their inner eye on the card on the table. The most talented of these 'seers' are able to visualize and correctly identify the card, time and time again. They do this by entering into that room with their photonic eye and literally viewing what is on the down-turned card._

This study confirms that our universe adapts to what presents itself as holographically viable, meaning it will reveal what is there in terms of what is visiting that room, what is available within that space and time, and what is possible or not possible from the location that the person is focusing from, depending on their personal power. These are the first stages of induced remote viewing.

People have struggled for many years to understand and harness this capacity so that it can be controlled and reproduced on command. But remote viewing can't be accurate one hundred percent of the time, for it's not a faculty that is meant to be controlled. It will arrive upon your path naturally in correspondence with your personal power as a human being.

What I am outlining here might sound contradictory, since those remote viewers are getting results. This would seem to indicate that their personal power must be at the point that they can summon this capacity at will. While this is initially the case, once they have exhausted their resources by forcing the amount of precious energy that they have saved to view and retrieve the information of what's on a card in another room, then their photonic viewing capacity will diminish by degrees and the eventual spontaneous expression of this faculty won't occur for them.

When solicited, remote viewing becomes a mechanism that is infused with one's conscious perception of this world. Thus the dimensional communication received is tainted due to the fact that practitioners are forcing their third eye to see a second attention fixation, in order to move and manipulate or adjust this world in accordance with their will. Now, 'in accordance with their will' is very, very important.

Bill:

What do you mean? They are forcing it?

Lujan:

Yes, because they are seeking a desired outcome. Now, you can only do this so many times until the element of interference takes over and seeing becomes something totally structured around what one wants and no longer composed of what's necessary. This brings a great detriment to the human's innate ability to remote view in a fashion that is timely to the ebbs and flows of Spirit. This interdimensional access is something that we are meant to arrive at naturally as our personal power demands that we recognize that elusive part of ourself, in comparison to Spirit, so that we can begin to clearly see.

Once a person believes that they have total control over their seeing, the will becomes a tool of the first attention, a mechanism that is employed to manipulate the environment. By remote viewing with an agenda, they are unwittingly violating that space and time that they go into. This is why a lot of remote viewers don't succeed in progressing beyond their initial goals; they are diverging from their true path by virtue of the fact that this application of seeing has everything to do with control and nothing to do with heart. It is very important to understand and take into account that when remote viewing, one is using one's photonic energy.

Bill:

What exactly do you mean by photonic energy?

Lujan:

Photonic energy is your luminous potential and is the same vital resource you use to go into a dream. When somebody says they are going to develop their energy Double in dreaming, what they are actually doing is exercising their photonic awareness, which is their bio-electromagnetic reserve, projected from their heart to their third eye matrix. This perceptual faculty that traverses through its witnessing has multidimensional characteristics. If used in dreaming, the danger is that this potential, this perceptual layering, can be captured and exploited by entities in the second attention.

If a warrior wants to achieve power, it is their desire - which translates into a need - that can be catered to. When catering occurs, one's clarity and power are drawn into a vortex of self-serving justification that is mirrored back as the false achievement of the warrior's potential, which is begging to be validated through that reflection. This is how our photonic, bio-electromagnetic resource can be used against us.

Visions of an ego-gratifying nature do not belong to the energy Double that a seer develops in this world. In fact, the Double is not something to develop, since it is already here. You become aware of it by virtue of the fact that it makes itself available to you, and for everyone this manifests differently. The Double is an unknown factor that cannot be interfered with, neither from a socially-determined viewpoint nor from the seer's perspective.

The trap within modern approaches, as in ancient sorcery circles, is the notion that one must utilize the first attention by going to sleep and entering into the second attention – dreaming – with one's third eye, the same photonic awareness used for remote viewing. This practice is based on the idea that you are going into dream constructs to develop your energetic self and verify that you are progressing as a warrior.

What's wrong with that is that you are using up your photonic energy to travel into these realms. What's more, once you venture there, that reality contains you as a foreign position that is not quite in accordance with your living world, or the first attention, which you are sleeping in.

Exploring dreaming has become more popular since the release of the sorcery writings that emerged in the 1960s. Warriors were informed that they would forge their energy Double by entering into the second attention lucidly. The truth of it is that your Double is drawn to the focus of your photonic energy in the waking world. The usefulness of dreaming in the process of awakening is that it is a way to activate the conscious awareness of your photonic eye, which introduces the seer to dimensionalization as an experiential possibility.

What needs to be questioned here is the wish to create oneself as a photonic projection in other realms. You have to understand that this holographic counterpart is not your 'Energy Double', or 'The Other', as you may have heard it referred to. Even using the term 'Energy Double' is misleading, so I will just refer to it as the Double. The Double functions independently of our lives, yet is interdependent and indispensible. We need each other.

The reason fledgling warriors are asked to go into dreaming is to learn to become involved in viewing their dream imagery, and then subsequently enter into an alternate dream scene, and so on and so forth. If they are careful and do not fall under the influence of inorganic entities, this will trigger the neurological process which is connected to the release of DMT (dimethyltryptamine) from the pineal gland; thereby activating that internal visual matrix that is the doorway to our true human potential within dimension.

This process is not dissimilar to an initiate being introduced to hallucinogenics, in that each undertaking, while offering unprecedented new possibilities, also has the potential to possess the warrior in comparison to their emerging, as yet undeveloped power. Hallucinogens within themselves have entities attached, as does dreaming, though in the beginning this may not be apparent.

It is crucial to know when to withdraw so as not to be led too deeply into the labyrinth, which can lead to losing our independence through borrowing the awareness provided. If we step too far into either reality accessed, our natural fractalization will be tainted by the influence of the entity that possesses the hallucinogen, or the scout that may engage us within dreaming.

Let's get back to the subject of using our photonic energy to traverse other realms. Upon entering dreaming, you arrive into one compartmentalized aspect of that reality. This construct, while you are there, is as solid and as real as the world you live in. You travel upon your own luminous reserves to get there.

Sometimes you may contact other energy forms and find yourself in their domain, communicating with them. The reason you can see or communicate with these other types of awarenesses is that your luminosity magnetizes them. Once you attract these beings, they connect and interweave their energy with yours. This causes you to actually bring a part of them back with you and leave a part of yourself there. The effect of this is that you will never be the same again. Even though this is a consequence of living your life, it may or may not be apparent to you how you have changed. And this within itself is dangerous, for it blocks your ability to reflect upon what or who you are in the moment you arrive upon.

When you attempt to go back to the reality that was constructed for your awareness, the presiding entity becomes dependent on communicating with you through your photonic energy. The first scene you went into was something you could see, and this construct was sustained by your photonic potential.

In other words, it uses your precious reserves to manifest the reality that you are witnessing. Once that is in place then co-dependence is established between the two beings. But is that useful for you? Is it viable for your energy to be deployed in this way? And what process does that symbiosis really instigate? Unfortunately you won't find out until you're on your deathbed.

The old sorceric way was to go into a dream and use the principles of stalking to solidify that reality. The concept of 'stalking' here refers to entering into an alternative construct to establish that site as a point of reference and to then use your applied will to attempt to re-establish it as a future event. Though this is what appears to be happening, it is actually impossible to achieve due to the fact that the site has been constructed for you, not by you.

You will instead encounter a new dream scene that will be forged in correspondence with the energy that you have been in contact with. The first dream scene you entered, the holographic site where you initially encountered the entity, will no longer be accessible. But the photonic energy that you used to get there will be anchored and utilized as a position to attract you, not to the original location but to the entity.

These scenes that are created and maintained with your personal power are designed to enthrall your attention. The inorganic will then maneuver in comparison to what you bring to the circumstance so that you may be kept focused. In essence, you are the one being stalked.

A lucid dreamer may be involved in this activity hundreds or thousands of times. When a warrior experiences the illusion of co-creating these scenes, this incites a desire for return. This very intention is what causes your photonic energy to remain in the dream realm. What is so dangerous about this is that your will to be *here* must completely return to you, but becomes divided because of your wish to be *there*. Recklessly expending your photonic resource in dreaming amounts to making an offering of yourself on the altar of the inorganic awareness. It is a sacrifice of your very potential, a form of bloodletting to the vampirous entities that you have availed yourself to, for they feed upon your cravings, thereby pilfering your essence.

The wish to return, which you perceive as yours, is the entity's spell to draw you back so that you leave more of yourself behind every time you go there. The dilemma is that you are being true to the entity instead of being true to yourself, though what you encounter so closely resembles you that the distinction becomes very difficult to make. The photonic energy that you leave behind is meant to be gathered in your heart center, amassed as your emerging potential as a warrior. When Juan Matus warned about being careful in dreaming, this is the risk that he was referring to.

It has also been said that you go into dreaming to obtain whatever you may need to sustain yourself in this world. However, it is more than likely that what you bring back may be an energy that is not compatible with this reality. This can distort the view of the warrior who is not resolved. Unresolved elements will perpetuate themselves through interactions that will be indirect and emotionally charged. Such enactments will not be governed by a warrior's true heart potential, due to the fact that they are routinely entering worlds that are not viewed by anyone else, using their internal eye to travel there. This breeds secretive possessiveness, which in turn is covertly applied to the world at large.

Upon this trajectory, the seer becomes self-centered and selfishly absorbed by their own sense of grandeur. Obviously their intentions are infused with their desire for power in the waking world, since they have the illusion of power in the world where they sent their photonic potential. When that person emerges from the dreaming reality into the first attention, the connection that their photonic energy has with that realm will cause them to be subtly saturated with that resonance. Thus they will start to operate with the more refined, socially-determined principles of stalking that indirectly have been applied to them in the reality that they immersed themselves in. In plain terms, this means they will maneuver and manipulate the environment around them to position it so as to obtain the most beneficial outcome for them. These actions do not have the integrity that they may seem to have. Do you understand, Bill?

Bill:

Yes, I think I do.

Lujan:

Good. Now you are putting the pieces together on your own. We are all searching for authenticity in terms of what will reveal the unknown factor within ourselves.

We haven't yet fully discussed the Double. We have been conversing about the energy that warriors send into the dream realm, but to reiterate, this is not our Double; it is our photonic potential. The Double is comprised of the hundreds of thousands of positions that are localized within one awareness, which have to do with our luminous energy being witness to different compartmentalized realms of the universe. These positions become the access points of the warrior, revealing their proclivities in terms of their abilities as a seer. This is a more accurate way of describing what is known as 'the assemblage point'.

When the Double integrates, this activates the conscious assimilation of the phenomenon just outlined. This amalgamation is how we establish our link with the multiple interactivity of our true human potential within dimension, which is connected to our many lifetimes, and is also interwoven with the wisdoms of other seers' lifetimes.

The most pertinent of what has been learnt throughout a lifetime of these fluctuating anomalies will be accessed upon one's ultimate physical departure, unlike in the case where prolonged interaction with inorganic awareness has been pursued, whereby these memories will not be made available to the seer at the moment of their death. Instead one's memories will be possessively consumed via this contact, leaving the warrior stranded and then reborn without access to the interlinking wisdoms of their third eye process to fortify the recommencement of their evolution. Thus the perpetual cycle of feeding upon one's photonic potential continues.

Once you begin to understand the intricacies of the Double's integration, then the allegory of the assemblage point becomes absolutely valid. It is not a ball of energy floating somewhere behind your back. This metaphor was given as a didactic device to allow fledgling warriors to conceive of possibilities beyond their range. The multiple positions described refer to the fluctuating effect of the different influences that your photonic potential comes into contact with.

This concept, which was introduced to mainstream consciousness in the context of the stories of Juan Matus and his apprentice, was described in terms of a shift brought on by a physical blow from the Nagual that induces a heightened state of awareness. In reality the apprentice was not struck from behind to affect movements of his assemblage point; it is the mere presence of the Nagual that induces shifts of attention, which have to do with opening the channels of the multiplex that is our third eye process. This minor embellishment has misled modern-time initiates and caused them to fixate upon the description as a literal proposition, which was put forth to substantiate the possibility that perception can be altered through one's attention. In reality, it is the *release* of fixation that allows the possibility to shift from one dimensional matrix to another within the human domain.

When you go into dreaming, you are entering a highly sophisticated equation. Its adaptability aligns itself upon your entrance, before you even become conscious of where you have arrived, though it appears that the decision to be there has been initiated by you, the warrior.

Remember, dreaming is an ancient facet of attention, and you are endeavoring to traverse a well-worn trail that gives the appearance of a new frontier being arrived upon. Your comparatively infantile awareness will be supplied with whatever it is that will most effectively spellbind you. What you seek will be reflected back, and this gratification is so very important for catching your attention. As a result of being catered to, you become familiar with all those varied dreaming locations, containing layered information that is manufactured to correspond with the under-developed parameters of your present perception.

You will henceforth be delivered into a false feeling of achievement, which will be jealously defended in the first attention, through arrogant assertions that become the controlling factor that revolves around an over-developed intellect. This highly manipulative influence belongs to that very old aspect of the universe that must be avoided at all costs, for it is not concerned with your personal progress but only its own input into the direction your journey takes, and into the luring of other humans, so they too will come and share their photonic energy.

This ancient intention supplies warriors not with wisdom that will give them freedom but bait that will trap and ensnare them and further inflame their need to be in control and to be absolutely right, without question. Are you beginning to see why this path is so very dangerous?

When Juan Matus gave this information to his apprentice, his apprentice in turn created the majority of the writing on this subject. Over the years, this body of work has been widely appropriated as a belief system. It is this very doctrine, which is purported to bring freedom, that unfortunately now loops in on itself as a fledgling seer's social eddy.

When a warrior whose luminous resource has been spent in dreaming dies, he or she will not have the possibility to amalgamate all of these diverse positions into one focused reality, which is the culmination of all their life's input. All of their photonic energy, which emanates from the heart center and is our most precious resource, has been possessively utilized elsewhere, leaving that warrior bankrupt at the most crucial point, their inevitable end.

When you live whole-heartedly in this reality and utilize your body consciousness to define your living perception within the waking world, your bio-electromagnetic energy will amass through your purposeful self-determination. Then you will realize that you don't need to depend upon entering into unknown territory to forge your personal power.

Lots of people defend the idea of going into dreaming because it's in the Native American tradition, or it's in this or that shamanic culture. While this is so, a warrior must *wait* for visions to manifest and patiently abide by those messages that will become true indicators in alignment with the dictums of Spirit.

You will eventually have the capacity to interpret what arrives by virtue of the gravity that is your power in this world, and you will transmit the realities of these insights with those people who are around you.

When we share our visions, that insight transports itself into this reality and the photonic energy that has erupted from within us is given communally. The community will see the truth and knowledge in the vision, for it will be real and not contrived through desire. This mutual enrichment will be accomplished through the fact that you did not seek to go into dreaming, yet visions occurred as a natural consequence of your evolution and a true manifestation of your personal power.

This is how one's photonic journey becomes a process of real seeing and thus integrates with our third eye potential, in correspondence with the active realization of our heart path. As one's power grows, so will their precognitive abilities. This will happen naturally when you are centered here in this world and nurturing your photonic energy in your heart center, to blossom and be shared communally. This will manifest as visions that appear outside the body, as a holographic overlay superimposed upon the everyday world that presents itself in accordance to the power of the receiver.

Your Double will nestle when your bio-electromagnetic energy vibrates at a higher frequency, but unfortunately this can't be pre-empted. It simply approaches as your personal power becomes stronger. However, if you are using your photonic energy to create a dreaming replica of yourself, then your Double will not have any possibility of integrating with you within the waking reality, where your true potential exists.

Your Double is multifaceted, as dreaming is, but in a totally different way. When you die in this world and you fully contact your third eye process and your multidimensionality, everything will amass upon a point of no arrival in the space of bardo, in between lives. If you have lived your life with power, all your most pertinent memories will be returned to you.

The only path that has any meaning is one that resolves your being in the feeling that your heart is empowered by doing what is necessary for your existence. We cannot afford to waste our potential in attempting to establish our power within dreams. As you know, in the second attention you have to be so careful not to be drained of your resources. I know you have experienced this, Bill. In your dream, you were walking around with no pants on, but it was only at the moment you spoke that you were pounced upon.

The resonance of your voice has been established in your heart center. Once you speak in dreaming, the frequency – which is your true photonic signature – becomes immediately apparent. The reason for this is that the base of your tongue is attached to your heart center, and this is the largest of the chakras.

The moment you use your voice the predator realizes, "There is our prey; we recognize him. That is photonic energy speaking and it belongs to Earth. That voice is connected to the personal power of a warrior who is here, displaced, and we have the opportunity to make this luminous being dependent on our ancientness."

They know how young and childlike we are; such a small, beautiful morsel, such a precious flame. That light, although fragile, is so powerful in its own right through the fact that we are going to die. We have such a limited amount of time to accomplish what we are here to do before our mere memory is relinquished in our own death.

You see, these entities don't suffer this problem. They are timeless and have existed as long as the universe has. All we know is that we encounter them and, once they are engaged with, we risk being captured, either through our own naivety, a lust for power, or simply because we were advised to go there. The purpose of this publication is to inform the warrior of that naivety, to reach into the complexity that is our desire for achievement, and transmit the understanding that dreams which provide the illusion of power are really not what we need to progress on our path.

The ancient cultures, the sacred knowledge and the indigenous peoples, are becoming extinct. The wisdom that belonged to humanity has all but been forgotten. Almost all truths pertaining to our dimensional potential have been eradicated. This precious knowing, crucial to our growth, has been extensively interfered with. The most central part of our self is being denied true expression and waylaid by our own species. This is not right. It seems that all the way from the powerful to the powerless, we are currently deadlocked within a corrupt, self-sabotaging paradigm that is in utter contradiction to our evolutionary path.

Why would one human being focus on another as something to corral or control unless their fundamental essence had been warped? Uncovering the core of this subject is very important in terms of enabling us to rejoice in our power. We must remember that the only true wealth we have is the freedom of another human, not their entrapment. Engaging this type of intention will draw to us the most precious resource we can come in contact with: Our Double.

The Double is composed of so much energy and information by virtue of the fact that it has access to the universe in ways we cannot yet comprehend as a species. If our Double merges with us, we then become infused with our capacity to be interconnected universally, where we witness ourself within dimension, yet we are one. Thus we are faced with the largest contradiction there ever is: We are at the source of everything, yet we are everywhere at once, which is the crux of the complexity of that labyrinth that is our true human potential. Upon the approach of the Double, our third eye opens. When the other truly integrates, we fan out, expanding into our own universal possibilities.

In 'Awakening the Third Eye', I mentioned that each human being has the capacity to operate with two, three, or four hundred energy compartments. These condensed units of information are the compartmentalized aspects of one's third eye potential.

When I use the word 'compartmentalized', I do not infer through this premise that there is separation. On the contrary, the third eye matrix within itself is absolutely unified. It's just that the personalized, momentary experience of these factors necessarily fluctuate in comparison to the circumstances that one arrives upon, thus producing the isolated anomaly, which is to be viewed, or completely missed. These unified singularities are the perceptual compartments that each human being possesses, which interlink beyond our wildest imaginings with every sentient being we've ever had contact with.

This multidimensional functionality incorporates past, present, and future events, which appear randomly to inform the warrior of their absolute connectivity. Compartments of our third eye process are sent out as scouts to contact future continuums which bear relevance but which will only appear as a precognitive informant if power deems it necessary. If not, the natural ebbs and flows of fate will confront the warrior without this forewarning companion. This particular faculty is also connected to previous lifetimes, which give gravity to the warrior's presence in terms of how they choose to conduct themselves in the moment.

I have experienced this as a jolt to my being, reminding me of something that I knew, yet in the same breath had forgotten. This in itself is shocking: To have the capacity to remember so much, yet be simultaneously utterly humbled by a randomly accessed event that contains information which propels one to steadfastly pursue the path of one's heart.

A state of constant perceptual flux allows multiple aspects of a seer's potential to manifest as a holographic overlay. This light-borne interactivity may show itself as an internal realization that has affixed to it an accompanying image. It can also come in the form of external holographic visual matrices that appear externally to be seen, or merely a bird that sings in our world, which relays a message that has our memory contained within it.

We all have different capacities in terms of our inner eye's ability to fan out into a vast perceptual net, composed of those two, three or four hundred connected units of information, comprised of futuristic and past memories that return to the moment to be reviewed. Our reviewal becomes stronger when the stories – which are the wisdoms of a warrior's life – are shared and thus connected as a multiplex of interchangeable perspectives.

One is not diminished, nor another elevated, because of the capacity one may have to access more compartments. It is only in the early stages of the path of awakening that the excess energy of a Nagual provides the appropriate energetic response for growth to occur. This initial boost will then become interdimensionally exchanged through the whisperings of Spirit, which thus become holographically interchangeable between light beings, within the vast medium that is the collective consciousness of our species.

In becoming collectively connected, we focus the true photonic potential of our third eye matrix, which is intimately linked with the wisdoms of our heart, upon the realities that appear in our waking world, the first attention. Thus we integrate our second attention capacity within this world, which then becomes our third attention potency to patiently wait for our true human Spirit to emerge. As this attention stabilizes, our Double simultaneously begins to travel towards us, gathering the necessary momentum. This alignment reflectively yields the true possibilities of our human potential and is opposed to the connectivity to inorganic pathogens which we have unwittingly assigned our attention to.

What actually takes place when the Double comes into close proximity is this: Imagine two magnets that are irreversibly attracted to each other, which represent you and your Double. At a certain distance, these polarities will inevitably collide. Upon that collision, the internal visual cortex is plucked like a harp string, and it will continue to resonate at a frequency comparable to the force of the impact. Thus the overall vibration is raised to a fourth-dimensional capacity. Upon the emergence of the core vortices of our true perceptual inheritance, the full ramifications of the seer's potential are awakened to the micro and macro cosmos, through the spiraling matrices of our universal attention.

This fourth dimensional integration from our Double gives us the capacity to receive information not only from the true holographic universe – which will interactively accommodate our human attention – but also from all of our past life experiences, which then become known collectively. This in essence is the fourth attention. This uninhibited universal communication, which will appear as pure insights to lead humanity to the pinnacle, is our rightful evolutionary state to be experienced.

Even though the path that I beckon you to follow through my words may seem difficult, merely hearing the syntactical explanation that truly belongs to our dimensionalization will begin an awakening. These words will enliven a second, third and fourth attention momentum that will bring the future to your moment, even if you don't initially realize that this may be occurring.

If you could possibly see it this way for me, just for a moment: When Columbus arrived at the shores of the Americas, the shaman had to focus for a long time to conceive of the fact that the strange boat in view could possibly exist. Having no reference point for this vision within their collective experience, it took all the energies of the indigenous people to allow the appearance to have any reality. As they became used to the sight, it became easier and easier for them to realize that more boats were coming. This is not unlike the paradigm shift we are preparing for now, within the parameters of what we believe or understand to be possible.

The only problem with this metaphor is that it refers to a solidified, first attention, collective memory which has been documented as our history. What I wish to do here is to beckon the memory of our future, which we have already visited, to be awakened in the mysteries of our moment that we patiently await to appear. Waiting is the hardest part of a warrior's journey.

When we interact with each other, as we all do on a daily basis, we combine the possibilities of our compartments. If we consider that we can create millions of permutations with only a handful of variants, imagine the potential combinations created by our several hundred compartments, or energy cells, multiplied by the several hundred cells of the next person, multiplied by every person we come in contact with, and all the people they come in contact with. The combinations are endless.

This unfathomably complex amalgamation is what is constantly happening with us as sentient beings. There are so many possibilities that belong to our human nature and to our existence, which we are meant to access and evolve towards. We are light beings waiting to wake up to the dimensionality of our universe and to our capacity to be interlinked on such a massive level that, when it happens, energy and information rushes in and the photonic intensity of our heart center floods our third eye. Thus we gain access to our fourth-dimensional matrix.

Even if we simply gaze at one another for the slightest moment, our compartments become combined. Every interaction entails a synthesis of our subtle fields of perception. This is where we get the endless energetic permutations that belong to our human experience, which then fan out as the interdimensional aspects of our true nature. Though this is within everyone's reach, most people do not fully attain this way of being, due to their Double not yet being close enough to them.

Bill:

So the Double is not a tool to be used, as it seems to be suggested in other works? Those teachings suggest that a shaman would use it to be in two places at once, or to strike and injure someone from a distance, for example.

Lujan:

It is extremely unusual that someone has the capacity to send their Double. Even though this is something I have learnt to do through the techniques I have obtained, it very rarely occurs. Juan Matus and the old Nagual Lujan had the ability to travel intentionally on the awareness of the Double. It usually happens very late in life when one has the wisdom and fortitude to handle the power obtained.

It must be understood that the Double is not something to be controlled. In most cases it acts of its own accord, independent of the wish of the warrior. It has been alluded to in popular sorcery writings that a seer can be in this reality and simultaneously in another position, and be cognizant of both sites. I can confirm that it is possible to be conscious in two places at once, viewing the activity of one's Double – which is actually seeing the circumstance viewed through the Double's eyes – but again, it is extremely rare, even for a seasoned warrior.

The only way to really comprehend or experience the Double is to endeavor to stabilize the gravity of your life path so that your personal power is centered and not waylaid or dispersed. This is how to beckon the Double and start to perceive things within dimension.

As you begin to reinstate your interdimensionality, your internal pictures, dialogue, and normal dreams will dramatically diminish, and you will access your awareness of external pictures that bestow wisdom. All your senses will deliver you information. You will become self-sufficient through the experiential, universal connectivity that directly avails itself to you.

At this juncture, your true voice becomes fully active and you begin to speak other people's realities, to alleviate the burden of their life so they can start to express their own truths. I will use a word here I don't use often, but you start to resolve their 'karma' for them. By addressing their karmic challenges you take away their illusions. You remove their fundamental fantasies by reaching beyond the façade of their perceived isolation and communicating directly to their innermost self.

The assumption that we are all safely screened off in our own private world is one of the first barriers to be relinquished. Coveting pseudo-privacy is not beneficial for anybody, for under this delusion, we are neither completely here nor there. What's more, within this premise, true inaccessibility, which is the mystery of the moment, will not be accessed. I know this sounds like a contradiction, but you will come to terms these very elusive factors eventually, upon your path.

When one's photonic energy is absently deployed elsewhere, for example enthralled within the second attention, or preoccupied within the dramas that ensue in the first attention, one will never realize the gravity to sustain the approach of the Double. Upon a divided foundation, which in essence is so complex within its subtle variants, the ultimate attunement of our fourth-dimensional matrix will not occur.

How could we possibly communicate sincerely as a species if we are fully involved in upholding an illusion of what we perceive to be our authenticity? Truth is in the room when we speak from our heart.

The most potent and unhindered perception occurs when our mind is switched off and pictures appear in front of our eyes, like holograms, for just a split second. True information will be revealed in this imagery. Then when we communicate we grow from that exchange or transmission, as it originates from the authenticity of our visions.

When the truth of our interconnectivity is undeniably established, the fourth-dimensional aspect of our communal wisdom will be realized. Once this affects more than one percent of our populace, our collective journey will truly begin.

That is why I said to you in the very beginning that when you saw Mescalito, you should have absorbed that vision, not lived it through someone else's teaching by screaming and running at it. Their reality, which wasn't the truth for you, became a cognitive distortion, by you stepping through that example as an instruction regarding what you should do as a warrior. This kind of mimicry is not a viable option for a sovereign being. The truth is that *you* saw it. What that vision was giving you was the realization that you have the ability to see something external, something beyond the first attention. The question is: What can you do with it?

Instead of asking yourself that, all of a sudden the programming of another sorcerer's teachings took over, which are so similar to the doctrines of a socially governed world that all you were left with was branches and shadows.

This is the reason why we need to live within the truth of our heart and not the conventions that become the accepted premise that one's consciousness abides by as the pseudo-truth of their circumstance, which is an illusion. Thus you lose yourself and your true authenticity, in turn making yourself unwittingly accessible through a first attention fantasy, even though you didn't realize it.

WAITING

Bill:

I have been contemplating the subject of waiting lately. I hear you and other teachers say that you must wait patiently and know what you are waiting for. It seems to me that you can never truly wait for anything. If we just sit here and wait, nothing happens.

I am in business for myself and if I don't attempt to get something done then I will go bankrupt. I can wait for the major events, but how do I wait on a day-to-day basis and put this theory to practice? I feel like I have been cast out to sea and if I stop treading water, I will certainly drown.

Lujan:

You have to keep trying, in terms of releasing your need to want to be waiting. That's it. You have to keep going until you get a result. That outcome will point you in the next direction and lead you to the next step. You have to wait while you project forward your goals and your resolve. It is essential to wait in a way that neutralizes your feelings of futility, for this is a socialized mechanism to keep you perpetually engaged, when, in fact, inactivity can be equally as powerful.

Even though all actions are ultimately futile in terms of their inevitability, there is meaning when one truly applies oneself to the essence of a circumstance. Once the input of your attention has been fully given to that activity, one must immediately withdraw investment, to allow power to apply itself to the warrior's empty perspective. The selfless command of one's intention yields true pearls of wisdom, the treasure of a seer.

The way to proceed is to realize that power is contained within the elusive moment that escapes the warrior while he waits. Patiently attend the accumulation of power to deliver the resources to do what you need to do and what you want to do. What you want to do won't be what you used to need to do, but it will be what you have to do. The paradox is that you are now doing what you have to do, so that you can get to do what you want to do.

Bill:

I think I understand what you mean, but I have found myself getting frustrated lately in the lack of results in my life. Seems like I'm always waiting, for money, or business, or progress, or something.

Lujan:

Waiting is a very unique skill for a warrior to master. You and I are doing it right now. We are waiting for a moment to arrive upon, yet the conclusion that awaits us is already facing us at this very point, we just can't push it. You are waiting and so am I, and in the midst of our waiting, look what's happened.

Bill:

Not a damn thing, best I can tell. I'm still stuck in the same place and waiting.

Lujan:

That's not true at all, Bill. What has happened in between the lull of our lives is the elevation of both of our awarenesses. The waiting and the getting together to have this conversation create so much energy and interest that this has caused us to fuse our destinies. It also generates momentum that fuels your positivity toward what you would normally see as impossible to achieve.

There is an interest or a fire in your heart for the information we discuss here. Without this fire in your heart, you would not be able to look at this empty page that has nothing written in it as you're waiting for it to write itself. While we are waiting for it to manifest, we have contacted each other and here we go. Waiting has created the appropriate moment for us to communicate. The positive response of our communication means we are compelled to explore subjects that have meaning for us.

When you have energy delivered to you, you are fully centered within the meaning of your own life, which is the only viable way to live as a warrior. Once this energy accumulates and becomes strong enough, you will try again, waiting for something to arrive, but you will do so with power and interest, not boredom and frustration. What you are waiting for is continually arriving; while at the same time, there is something you are acting upon within your waiting. What you don't realize is that you *are* getting what you're really waiting for. The extension of this is that the byproduct of what we are communicating here will create something more substantial in your life. We are generating energy for both of us and for our communal future.

LOVE AND LUST

Bill:

You once told me about a technique that involved drawing up your perineum to gather the electromagnetic energy around you. You only briefly mentioned this and then we changed the subject. You also cautioned that this is potentially a dangerous technique. Would you elaborate on the topic?

Lujan:

Yes. There is a technique for gathering energy through the palms of the hands and the soles of the feet. This is done by drawing up or tightening the perineum, which is the area between the rectum and the testicles or the vagina. In the future I will write a book about the traditional Oriental uses of this part of the physiology, for it is a vast subject. Essentially these kind of techniques awaken our sensitivity to chi, and the vital energy centers in the body. This awareness was common knowledge in our past, which as you know, has been all but eradicated.

You must be very careful using such techniques as they can have negative effects if misused. If you use it to forcibly attempt to draw energy from another person, all you will bring to yourself is darkness. This will result in a very unlucky path for you and can also cause serious health issues for the people around you.

I know a shaman that made his family members very sick by misapplying these methods and befell terrible ill fortune, himself. It can even cause birth defects if the practitioner has children after having practiced like this for a while. Energetic theft of this kind is a very ancient and dark practice that should be left in the old world with the rest of these types of traditions. They do not propel humanity toward freedom as a whole. We must evolve past such behavior. There are no shortcuts to true power.

Tantra is another discipline that can follow the path of base manifestation if not used correctly. Tantric methods have become almost exclusively associated with sexuality, especially in the West, and are widely misunderstood. Tantric practices are very common in the Balinese culture but, when used in the ways most often cultivated there, all they amounts to are attempts to manipulate the environment and bend everything to one's will with magic. This is what Tantric practices are reduced to, unless someone reaches the height of this art and then they learn to leave this way alone.

Many civilizations have gone through these phases of development, and this cultural dilemma is exactly what the Balinese are traversing at this point in their history. There are too many people playing with the fundamentals of magic whilst remaining fully dualistic and combative, instead of being totally one with each other. Anyone caught up in this kind of enactment has yet to understand that forcing one's will on the environment only corrupts those surroundings into something unnatural and, by nature, unpredictable; the very opposite of what was sought in the first place.

As I said, Tantric and similar schools of knowledge have become corrupted through incomplete and distorted appropriation. The practices of Kama Sutra and all of the sexual positions to open up the meridians and so forth have been widely adopted, but in a superficial manner which remains utterly divorced from the deeper implications that parallel the physical or rudimentary aspects. These popularized versions of the ancient wisdoms are not well defined enough to lead people to be self-empowered and genuinely driven from the heart center.

If you are energetically propelled from your sexual center, it is said that it will eventually bring love to your heart. The problem is that most people get caught in their lower centers through lust and interpret it as love; but where is the devotion and becoming fully immersed in union? How can you become totally at one and fully surrender to love when you identify with lust? This is a very difficult path for people to follow, for it finishes in the dead-end street of loneliness.

In many cases the gurus that teach these particular practices are driven by their own selfish agendas. The agendas don't appear to be obvious, since people are so easily caught up within the devices of their own self-serving intentions. Thus they are readily led away from the truth of what is really going on, as their desire for personal validation is stronger than their better judgment.

Bill:

What are the agendas?

Lujan:

Usually to have sex with young women; for instance, when gurus teach sexual freedom. Obviously they are going to advocate this if sex is their agenda. They may tell you that if your wife wants to go have sex with other men you have to let her, and then you have to deal with the emotions that arise from that. What a load of crap. This just causes undue stress and focus on something that is not really necessary.

We are made to be monogamous. We are truly not meant to intend this kind of division in our lives, as it creates turmoil in our hearts on a very deep level. Next the guy will go off and have sex, and the girl will have to go through all of the same negative emotional responses because she has lost her security within the boundaries of intimate trust.

Behind it all, the guru just wants to have all the sex he can. So he teaches this, and then he can pick the juiciest morsels for himself. Now he will say that you have to go through your upheavals to learn about yourself. You don't need to provoke unnecessary turmoil to know yourself. You just live your life as purely and simply as possible, because that is the only thing that really works. Anything else is primitively complex.

As a race, we must move beyond the premise of desire and gratification as the basis for our choices. In some cases, the importance of our sexuality becomes so distorted that we build practices around it. Again, this is primitive behavior. All it boils down to is creating a belief system that justifies getting what one wants, which is not always what one needs. In reality, this approach only suits the selfish.

Many people have become caught up in this type of conduct due to being all revved up on a sexual level by advertisements, TV, and a sex-driven society in general. When these people get into their sixties and seventies, everybody cools down and the sex drive diminishes. It is at this point that they will want to know where their beloved is. And where is their beloved? There is no monogamous partner to stand by them and say, "Here I am." They lived their lives with sexual choices and, when they are older, they don't have those same options, and the choices that were made come back as lonely incompleteness.

You have to live the way you are going to end up. You have to live within your heart, within your monogamy, and within the boundaries of your loyalty to your partner, which creates the harmony that necessitates union.

We must not react to each other's imprinted awareness, but love each other through our insecurities so that these very inadequacies are dissolved. Through love, caring attention, and patient understanding, we come to true security within ourselves. You can't tease someone's insecurity out to the surface by challenging them to go have sex with another person and then demanding that they remain balanced in the emotional maelstrom this provokes.

Bill:

Well, besides the sex with the guru part, I think you are describing most of modern society.

Lujan:

True. We must remember that within physical intimacy, what is taking place is a very deep exchange. When two human beings touch skin, there is a transfer of proteins, and through this familiarity, an energetic bond begins to formulate. Due to this biological factor the union gets stronger as the years go by. We are like doves, searching for that one true love.

TWILIGHT

Bill:

I have been doing some of the meditation techniques that you taught me in the past. I have noticed that I get the most bizarre results when I do this around sunset. I have also noticed that my interactions with entities and things of that nature also seem to be the most frequent around that time. Other shamanic writings seem to state that time of day or night is a special time. Is there anything to this or is it just coincidence?

Lujan:

It is as others have said: Twilight is the crack between the two worlds. It can be very dangerous since you are subject to the energy of the shifting light at that time of day. Twilight can confuse a person's perception. Most people need to stay still at that time, for if they have to move around, they stumble or fall easily. It is important to take care or avoid wandering about in the wilderness at dusk for that very reason. The eyes are normally programmed to see in the light and when the day transitions into darkness, the eyes take time to adjust. This transition can allow the world of power or the second attention to act upon a person much more readily.

The story you told me of the man in the hat was an example of this. You saw power present itself to you, yet you indirectly went to the vision by attempting to act upon it in the same way someone else was instructed to, which wasn't right for you. Did it work out? Not really. You should have known that that particular vision had a meaning for you; it was embedding a feeling of awe. That is what it has been ever since that point. You have felt like there has been a presence continuously on the periphery of your awareness, something pending.

MEMORY

Lujan:

I was doing some shamanic healing on someone once when he told me a story of when he was a child. He said that he had a faint memory of being very young, maybe two or three years old. He could remember being in the back seat of a car, when his father and another man got out and took a dead body out of the trunk and dumped it in a swamp. The body was wrapped in sheets. This person, now a man, told me it took many years to come to grips with this, but that he had lived all his life with the strangest feelings of guilt and apprehension whenever he thought of that scene.

Bill:

If this person was so young, how did he know what was really going on? How did he know that these people weren't just taking out the trash?

Lujan:

Children always know. Knowing comes through the skin, which is the first gate to dreaming awake. Through the skin, we feel and know information. This person knew what was going on and had absorbed the guilt and apprehension from the people around him. I know he wasn't lying to me when he told me the story, for a child not only feels what happens around them, their comprehension is unfiltered since they don't yet have a socially-determined perspective.

As a child, you see the gestures and you perceive the intentions so acutely portrayed in every single movement. You understand the language of those movements because that's all you know. The feeling is attached to you and it pulls on your being, adjusting you to receive what is going on and, in the same breath, demanding that your body conform to the situation of other people's way of being, which is often distorted and ugly because they're not real. As a child, the world is mysterious and wonderful and, at the same time, harsh and frightening.

Have you ever seen a child when someone goes up to it and says, "What a cute little thing," and it starts crying?

Bill:

Sure.

Lujan:

It's due to the fact that the one who has approached is probably so twisted within themselves that the inner workings of the baby feel the pull of that person on its being. That baby doesn't experience the person trying to get them to conform to the social act of being cute. The baby receives the residue of that person's life, all the way up to the point of contact. The child is warped by the pressure of that person's journey. I would scream too.

Bill:

Dogs and animals act the same way, don't they? That's why they become skittish around some people. They can sense that person's life path.

Lujan:

That's right. The lesson here is to bring our awareness back to where we were as children. Babies are born into this world as seers. We need to become clean and clear, like we were children again. We need to see the world around us without the noise of the internal dialogue and our social programming. Children have an inherent ability to know what's occurring within their surroundings.

WITNESSING THE DOUBLE

Bill:

What is the link between the dreaming body and the Double?

Lujan:

There is a correlation between them, but it's not what you might think. The key to their connectivity is the heart chakra. Our Double can view through a perceptual aspect of our third eye matrix, which is the photonic eye's projection within dimension; yet is rendered powerless to intervene when the second attention fixation becomes solidified through inorganic influence. I will go into further detail about what that means later on.

It is the photonic eye itself that gains the power of the Double's influence when the Double comes in close proximity to the warrior. This is when our full potential magnifies as a multidimensional consciousness within the human domain, instead of being reduced to the narrow window view provided by inorganic attention, which in essence is but a flattened reflection of our human nature.

Just to make it crystal clear, your photonic eye, which manifests in dreams, is not your Double. When you live your life with power, you bring the Double closer to your physical body.

Bill:

How will we know when our Double is approaching?

Lujan:

Your Double will be seen by others when it is about ten to thirteen feet away from you. The way it happened for me on one occasion is that I was outside doing Dragon's Tears, while my wife was inside doing yoga. She looked out the window, to where I never practice, and saw me performing the movements. She watched me for two minutes, wondering why I was there, for she knew I didn't want to be viewed by the neighbors. Then a movement caught her eye and she glanced to the opposite window, about thirteen feet away, and saw me practicing where I usually do. She quickly looked back and my Double had disappeared. She relayed this story to me when I came back inside. This is one of the ways that you can verify that your Double is approaching.

Bill:

What else happens when our Double approaches?

Lujan:

We no longer dream in a familiar way, but we experience déjà vu and our precognitive abilities come to the surface. We gain access to our multidimensional abilities to be universally displaced, yet centered absolutely within ourself. Like a receptor, receiving information simultaneously upon the point of transmission, we speak those fractalized memories received, instantly recapitulating every aspect of ourself, yet only retaining the most viable elements pertinent to the present circumstance. Our wisdom avails itself in comparison to what can be known in the moment we arrive. We are so mysterious, so complex.

It is truly a shame that the warrior's way has been diverted so extensively, drawing seers into dreaming constructs that are as equally consuming as the social milieu. Warriors erroneously attempt to escape their full responsibility within the waking world by entering into those all-consuming alternate realities, which cater to those same social boundaries that bind them to the limiting parameters of the first attention.

Seen from this perspective, it is so very important to understand that it is the concentrated potency of our photonic potential that draws the mysterious phenomenon of the Double to us. As it gets closer and closer, it reveals itself, within the inexplicable nature of its traversing. When we assimilate the energy that exudes from this entity, it becomes us, enigmatically integrating within, to a non-locatable position.

Conversely, when social dramas and entity-driven attention in dreaming consume our photonic potential, this results in the Double becoming removed from us, in terms of distance from our central matrix. This is deeply detrimental, for it plays into the agenda of inorganic entrapment, which locks our awareness into absorbing labyrinths that, in turn, feed back as a distorted view into the world we live in. Thus we bind our reasonable faculties to the first attention and to our own sense of brilliance, which fosters a breed of intelligence that will never reveal the true heart of the matter.

When the Double is integrated, it becomes our truest ally, instead of being relegated to the outskirts of our awareness as a consequence of the calculated maneuvers of the predator to keep us separated from ourselves, from each other, from the universe and from our very multidimensionality.

When I met my Double, I absorbed enormous amounts of information about my personal circumstances. I also received a set of physical movements to be performed. The Double did not get up and show them to me; I received them through transmission, simply by being in its presence.

Bill:

Are those movements specific to you, or are they universal? Could they be passed on to others and still have the same effect?

Lujan:

The movements are not specific to me personally, but are aligned with the human chakra system. The unique coiling gestures are to awaken two specific chakras that beckon the Double. When it came, my progress was at that particular point at which I had enough personal power to sustain its presence and assimilate this information.

To answer your question more directly: Yes, I can teach these coiling movements, and they will have a similar effect on the practitioner, beckoning their Double to protect them against a predatorial onslaught, provided that their Double is close enough to begin with.

An example of the impact of what the Double's presence left me with, in terms of what I absorbed, was the lesson of closing the doors in one's life that have been left open. If you live in a round room, surrounded by doors, and you or someone else leaves one open, this will allow the wind in. The wind represents either energies from the world or aspects of human attention.

Whether you like it or not, if there is an opening, these elements will integrate, causing displacement of one's personal power by virtue of the fact that you have to deal with an enemy indoors, instead of viewing potential intruders or disturbances from an exterior perspective. This is the reason why all doors must be closed, so that a sneaky wind doesn't have the possibility to creep up on you.

We must attempt at all costs to keep our internal perimeters sealed. This lesson has to do with relationships between human beings and also being in harmony with the ebbs and flows of nature. Keeping this in mind will allow you to establish healthy boundaries around yourself. Such boundaries may not always make logical sense to all the people in your life, but you will limit unnecessary distraction and harm by closing doors that don't need to be left open.

Even if you stand centered in the middle of your circle, all those doors have to remain sealed. You cannot let anyone else enter, except for your beloved. The way you operate from this perspective is by seeing beyond the perimeter with your photonic eye, without leaving the nexus, for that area is your space and the boundary of your personal power. It is a very difficult thing to understand and master.

ENCOUNTERS WITH THE NAGUAL'S DOUBLE

This account was written by Leia and has been included here to further elaborate upon what occurs when one's Double is fully active and operational.

Leia:

I am making my way up a narrow path through green rice fields. A little stream flows briskly along to my left. The night chorus of crickets has given way to a loud call and response of roosters. They seem to remain unseen, like so much of Bali, behind a veil. It's one o'clock in the afternoon and I feel the warm sun overhead. I turn left onto a smaller path going to meet Lujan Matus. After crossing a tiny bridge I arrive at an archway. A black dog announces my arrival. Not wanting to upset the dog, I stay still, waiting. After a while Lujan appears, greeting me with a hug. The dog falls silent.

I perceive him differently from yesterday. He seems larger somehow. Massive even. I become aware of a pressure inside my chest. The feeling quickly enlists my abdomen, which I can feel tightening as I follow Lujan. We walk past some workers and little children playing amongst baby chicks and many plants. Beautiful birds are singing. I notice there is a very good feeling in his space. He motions me to sit down.

"What's going on?" he asks.

"Huh? Oh, I feel fine!" I respond with too much enthusiasm.

"You are different today. You have changed from yesterday. Your heart space is spinning differently," he relays to me, very matter of fact.

"Yeah." I turn my full attention to the unpleasant feeling swirling in my chest. "I am feeling somewhat nervous."

"Okay." He seems to welcome my comment.

"What is it?"

"I don't know," I say flatly.

"Yes, you do know. You must tell me what it is."

His pointed inquiry is increasing my anxiety. "It just happens to me," I begin, searching for words to fit the feelings. "When I perceive myself going beyond my limits, a fearful feeling begins to arise. It increases until I am subject to it. It surrounds me. It has happened my whole life."

"Where does it come from? What is its source?" He is regarding me intently.

"I don't know. I have just always had to deal with this. It comes up and envelops me as if it is a part of me." I can feel the hopelessness of my words.

"You know where it comes from" he insists. "Something happened to you. This thing is not a part of you. You did not have it yesterday. You were yourself completely. Now this has entered. Tell me what it is."

It appears I will have to answer. He is waiting, studying me. I want to escape his gaze. It feels as though he is reading my thoughts.

Nervous, I glance at him. He meets my eyes but I look away quickly, lowering my head. Gazing at the floor, I am suddenly in the hallway of my house when I was 15. My father is there, preventing me from going up the stairway. His presence is very oppressive and dangerous. I am cowering inside. He tells me he is going to break my spirit. I just look at him. I know he cannot do this, yet I feel my spirit move up within me and go out the left side of my body. I feel it hovering a little above me on my left. I become gripped with fear, knowing my spirit is out of my body. I am in a cold sweat. I am paralyzed.

"What is happening?" I hear Lujan's voice. It sounds far away.

I tell Lujan I know where the feeling comes from. I tell him about the encounter with my father.

"He is feeding off your energy" Lujan announces. It is more of a pronouncement.

"Right now?" I ask.

"Yes. When this site is triggered within you, he takes your energy. No one has the right to take your energy, Leia. This must stop immediately." He seems to be talking to my body. "You have to seal yourself." He falls silent and looks off to the side. Addressing me again, he says he can see visually what was occurring. He describes a chest of drawers. Some of the drawers are pushed in, making my energy available for taking. He tells me that now the drawers are going to go back into their proper position.

A picture flashes in front of Lujan as he speaks. The picture contains images that describe my energetic situation, and its resolution. Within the images is information, conveyed as feelings being sent directly to my heart center. The pictures transmit to me a feeling of how to seal my energy body. They also show me my energetic body sealed in an original state. The feeling is transferred to me, bodily.

"You just saw the pictures in front of us, didn't you?" He knows the answer.

I confirm that I saw.

"What appeared in front of us confirms that you are now sealed." As Lujan speaks, the tattoos on his forearms lift up a foot and hover there. It feels like they are participating or making a statement. As they hover, I feel the echo of my own feelings, a tremendous surge of love within my heart. "Your tattoos," I point out to him. He is observing them in silence.

I look around the room. It is very dreamlike. I look at Lujan. His eyes hold me within their kindness. I look within them for a long time. He beckons me to travel there and I travel, into nothing. His eyes are filled to the brim with emptiness.

"Shall we begin?" He asks.

Begin? I wonder what he means.

"What are you thinking?" he asks. I stop to examine my thoughts. My brain feels inert. "I'm not thinking anything," I tell him. "Good," he says. "Power never presents itself to those who are accessible."

He motions me to a massage table in the middle of the room. I plop down, looking at the floor. A reprieve.

"Do you feel that?" His hands are on my shoulders.

"Yeah." It feels altogether unique.

"That is my chi." It streams in, circling to my feet and returning to my head. He withdraws his hands. "Can you sit up?" He is handing me a pair of headphones. "This will last about an hour. Just listen and relax." He leaves, going up a flight of stairs.

I hear the sound of rain. The room is womblike, a refuge, dimly lit with cobalt blue walls. It seems aware of itself. Protective. I allow myself to drift.

A sudden presence enters the room, startling me out of my solitude. It is a force that flashes through me. Opening my eyes, I am surprised to see Lujan standing on my right. It is Lujan, but not Lujan. There is something strange about him. Then he vanishes. There is no one there.

"How are you doing?" Lujan is walking in.

"I just saw you in the room a minute ago!" I blurt out, part confession and accusation.

"Really?" he asks, surveying me intently. "What did I look like?"

"You looked exactly like you, only bigger."

"You saw my Double," he says.

"Your Double," I repeat as a kind of joke. A windy feeling becomes a highway through my abdomen.

"I heard the noise outside and knew you were distracted, so I came down. My Double just got here first." For some reason I laugh, aware there is no point. Recalling the noise I had forgotten, it is now a vivid memory. My mind drifts, leaving my body there to face the situation. Lujan laughs. He stands in front of me, omnipresent. There is a bouncy feeling in my heart center and my limbs are buzzing. A part of me comes unhinged and roams out to meet him. It feels like going out to play as a small child.

He observes me closely, then pauses as if to make a determination on some matter. "Go ahead and listen to the soundtrack. I'll be back to check on you in a little while." He leaves me with a pat on the shoulder.

I replace the headphones. Loud splats of rain are coming down. I hear African chanting in the background and focus on it to distraction, obsessing about whether it is real or imagined. An internal trembling makes me fidget.

Suddenly the air in the room seems to rush past me, coming from everywhere. It is the speed of the movement that is so startling. I open my mouth to gasp but make no sound. There is Lujan again. It's as though he flashes into form for a second and then disappears. I stare at the empty space. Moments later Lujan is coming down the stairs. He walks over to me with a huge grin on his face.

"I saw you again." I hear my voice from within a tunnel.

"I know. You saw my Double again. No one has ever seen it so consistently like this before." He seems excited. "Take those things off so you can hear me," he taps on the headphones. "This is very interesting, very unusual," he continues. "You beckoned me and so I came. My Double arrived first. It is always ahead of me, or just outside waiting." He speaks to me as if revealing a secret.

"I don't remember calling you," I respond.

His laughter reverberates in the room. It's contagious. I giggle, feeling elated and ridiculous at the same time. "Is there African chanting on the rain soundtrack?" I feel high, stoned.

"You are having quite a day, aren't you?" He beams at me, not answering the question. "There's another ten minutes of sound. Do you think you can listen a while longer?"

I want to ask so many questions. I answer. "Yes."

"All right. Keep your eyes closed!" He leans in, emphasizing the word 'closed'.

Alone, I prop myself onto my elbows and look around the room, scanning and circling. Minutes pass. Nothing happens. Tiring of policing the circumstance, I close my eyes. Bells are ringing in the rain. The chanting ceases. A bird just outside the door sings out and light floods the room. I wonder if the door is open and consider looking but do not.

He is here again. The Double. I feel the rushing sensation and a flash of panic. I fling my eyes open. He is closer this time, standing at arms length. He vanishes.

I wait for Lujan. He never comes. The rain stops and a night chorus of crickets begin. The sounds bring a memory of last night. I am upstairs in the bungalow and awaken to the cricket's song. Climbing out of the mosquito netting, I go to the open window and look into the rice field. A small section of plants come alive for the wind while the rest of the field remains motionless, witnessing itself. The wind moves like water on the plants in a glow of moonlight, swishing and swirling the delicate tips of the stalks. Lujan enters.

"Very unusual." He seems contemplative. "Are you okay?"

"Yeah, I'm okay" I keep quiet about this last sighting of him. He takes the headphones, intently observing me. A lengthy silence ensues. "I know you saw me again," he says finally. "You called to me. My Double was there but I decided not to come down again to talk."

"Oh," I say. "That's okay." I saw myself 'calling' as he described and it dawns on me that he has seen me when I am not there, too.

I search for some words. "Nothing is hidden," he offers.

THE NEXT AFTERNOON...

"Look at me," I hear. Lujan is standing at my feet. The voice conveys a sense of urgency. "Take a look at what is in this room. See what is around you!" Lujan's face moves like a mirage. I realize that I am dreaming.

"Yes, I will." I reply. Inwardly I do not feel up to the task.

"Quiet! Don't say anything." He commands. I become alarmed by my circumstance, remembering he has previously instructed me on the uselessness of talking instead of acting. My words cannot substitute for doing the thing now, without mental interference. I am already at a disadvantage. I have lost time.

My focus turns to the room. I struggle for a foothold in my surroundings. A fluttering brushes my left side but I cannot see what it is. My eyes are useless but I can sense its identity. I recognize it as a kind of emotional feeling. It is formless. I want to tell Lujan, but he is moving and not receptive to words. He relocates around to my left and stands behind me. There is no time to turn around and view him. Many 'feelings' are gathering in the room. They advance towards me. I use my arms and hands in a brushing motion to sweep the sensations down and away as they present themselves. With great effort I achieve some success.

"Leia," I hear my name and awaken. "Leia," a voice again calls my name out loud. "I'm here," I reply. I am talking to myself. I hear the call of a gecko. Yes, I think to myself, I am awake now. Sitting up I look around the bungalow. My last memory is of lying down in the afternoon to rest. Night has come to the field. The plants are glowing under a blanket of mist, still warm from sunning themselves.

NIGHT GAZING SESSION ONE

I leave to go see Lujan. I find him sitting cross-legged on the path facing the field. I sit down. There is a full moon overhead. The cricket's opus is underway.

He directs me to look at a very bright star. "The big one there?" I ask. "Yes, that one," he affirms. I move forward to remove a telephone wire out of my line of vision to the star. Lujan adjusts himself in the other direction. "I want you to keep looking at the star. Just keep watching it."

After a few minutes, the star begins to shrink. "You see the star shrinking?" he asks. "Yes," I tell him. "Now it is almost gone, it is disappearing," he continues. I nod my agreement. "Now it is getting bigger again. It is forming an hourglass shape like it is going to split in two." He narrates exactly what I have seen seconds after I witness it. "All right. Now I want you to shrink it back to its original size."

I commence efforts to shrink the bulging star. I have no idea how to do this. It returns to its original size. "Keep watching it. Gaze directly into it." He doesn't miss a beat. As I watch, the star begins to weave to the left and then to the right. Lujan describes the movement. It weaves more drastically back and forth left to right until it is swaying like the pendulum on a grandfather clock. Lujan says as much. "It is moving faster now...tick tock tick tock," he keeps time with each swing. It quickens and shortens from side to side until the star is vibrating rapidly, then stops.

"Now let's have a look at the moon. This is a very powerful moon," he says. He guides me through a series of gazing maneuvers with the moon. He then directs me to gaze at a point below the moon. I lower my eyes. The moon begins to move up. It is rising in the sky. Then it stops. I am just about to say something when it starts moving again. It is swimming like a tadpole, quickly climbing up, then stops. It feels like my heart has climbed with it. My heart feels lifted, ascending with the moon. I turn my head to look at Lujan, wondering if he has seen. "Keep watching," he whispers. In a burst, it is on the move again, swimming quickly up. It seems it might disappear. It has gone up but also out, away from us, settling deep into space.

"Look at the star." He directs my attention back to the original star. "Do you notice anything?" he asks. I am still in awe over the moon. "Look at the position of the star," he coaxes. At first, I don't see anything. Then I notice the star is way back under the telephone wire. I distinctly remember the star was over the wire when I gazed at it. Its position has shifted dramatically.

I wonder if we have been out here for a longer time than I realized. "We have been out here for 10 or 15 minutes," Lujan answers my thought.

"What happened in the sky is a movement in the fabric of space."

NIGHT GAZING SESSION TWO

Lujan sits in the grass behind a little rise of earth and motions me to join him. He is in silence for a long time. My mind wanders. I look out over the rice field. I can see the lights of my bungalow and the shirt I hung out to dry after washing. There is no wind. The stream is making a splashing sound on the other side of the path. After a while, it begins to sound like music. "The stream is singing Om Mani Padme Hum," Lujan says, breaking his silence. "It would be good to just lie here all night, listening."

"Can you see my shadow on the tree?" he asks. I hadn't noticed it. In fact I didn't even notice there was a huge tree just a little ways in front of us. Lujan's shadow is positioned perfectly within it. He looks at me to make sure I see and focuses back on the tree. "I am going to make my shadow very still, very crisp," he informs me.

As I watch, his shadow seems to darken, forming a sharp outline of dark against the tree. It is clear, like a figure in black on white paper. There is something tranquil about the shadow. It gives me a feeling of confidence to look at it. Next, his shadow begins to vibrate and expand. It starts to move like an image on the surface of water that has been disturbed. He narrates exactly what I am seeing. His words disturb what I have told myself, that I imagined what I saw.

Something begins to move on his shoulder. His shadow seems to be growing there. Then something leaps out of his shoulder. It has the shape of a gopher popping out of a hole. It is very pronounced. Again, he verbally confirms what I have already seen.

"Let's switch places," he says, like we are playing a game. We trade places. He tells me to make my shadow move the same way his did. "Picture raising your arm above your head, but keep your arm relaxed," he coaches me. Nothing happens. After several minutes, I manage a small bulge from the top of my shoulder. "Make your shadow very clear and still." He switches my task. I watch my shadow become more solid with a clear outline. It appears calm and peaceful. "Now make your shadow vibrate," he commands. I look at my shadow and tell it to vibrate. It seems to work. I can see it vibrating. I receive a "good" from Lujan.

We switch places. Lujan tells me he wants to make flames come out of his shoulder. "No," he says, "I'm going to try something else." I watch his shadow intently, waiting to see what happens. Suddenly a light appears on his shoulder. It fans out like an accordion and drops down six or seven folds of light from the top of his shoulder. It finishes in a ball of light then evaporates into the darkness.

This time I'm sure I have imagined the effect. Again, like subtitles in a movie, he recites exactly what I have seen, narrating each detail. Very purposefully, he explains that he is corroborating what I have seen. In fact, he has confirmed everything I have seen.

THE NEXT DAY: LESSONS IN ABSORBING SILENCE

"Close your eyes." I realize I am staring at him. It is a simple request. "Listen to the music." For some reason, I wonder where this is going.

Lujan appears far away and giant at the same time, a sign I have come to recognize signaling shifts in awareness. I close my eyes and immediately feel myself being split. One part moves in stillness with the music while the other part sits, moved to distraction. The second part feels foreign, invaded by static. The duality itself feels strangely familiar. I sense I may have dreamed this way for a long time, lost to myself. My awareness ping-pongs between the two.

"Open your eyes. You can bring what you have captured within the music into this room." I hear him but don't believe this can happen. I feel if I open my eyes, I will lose the 'me' that exists within the music. As I open my eyes, the distracted me dissolves while the stillness expands, becoming my totality. The feeling is brand new. Nothing is out of place. The feeling is an absolute knowing within, reflected back to me from everywhere. Joy arises within me.

Lujan is smiling. "How do you feel?" I have no desire to speak. I am at peace. There is nothing happening all at once. I am happy gazing into my own 'being-ness'. "Are your legs buzzing?" he asks. They are buzzing. So are my arms, chest, and the top of my head. My whole body is buzzing. "Do you feel high?" Clearly I am very altered. I start to laugh. I am very high. It is a kind of elated lucidity.

"Look around the room. We are here, present but not interfering." He is right. There is no interference. Nothing, absolutely nothing is going on. Stillness exploding. I am at ease and possess a profound sense of wellbeing. I enjoy immensely the feeling of being inside my body. I can sense everything about the room and everything outside the room, and in the garden. Time stops to explain each moment.

In this moment, Lujan reveals many things about eternity, awareness, and the natural world. I know the truth of his words but do not have enough personal power to maintain the information in a linear way. He doesn't stop to ask if I understand. It feels like he is talking to my energy body as much as to my intelligence. I am able to listen intently without effort, receiving his words into my heart space. His revelations make me laugh out loud. Joy envelops me.

I ask Lujan if he altered my awareness by some means, or by transmission. He explains that although his presence is a catalyst, it is our neurotransmitters, which have a receptor site that welcomes naturally produced DMT from the pineal gland, which produces this state of awareness. He said that his benefactor took him and they traveled this way, in a bubble.

"I have been traveling ever since. I never came back. You don't have to come back. It is a choice. You can just keep going.

TIMES OF GREAT SORROW

Bill:

You mentioned 'times of great sorrow' in a lesson we once had. I meant to ask you about it then, but the subject changed. What did you mean by 'times of great sorrow'?

Lujan:

There are times in your life where you are faced with a difficult event. You may find that you are in trouble somehow, such as when going through problems with your health, or financial hardship. A loved one may be sick or dying, or you may have had an accident. You get put into a position where you reflect on the elements that are relevant or important for you in your life at that time, and you start to eliminate what is not good for you. It's just a natural process. You don't want to be focused on this when you have to be focused on that.

Times of great sorrow are when something will come and challenge you, which will seem to be going to defeat you in comparison to your innate purpose as a human being. For most Naguals or seers, there are times of great sorrow where really significant challenges make it more difficult to stay on their path. This difficulty is needed though, for it allows one to delegate energy to what are only the most necessary elements in one's life. This occurs because that energy can't go anywhere other than to what is essential, as there is no excess to deal with extraneous circumstances. Even though a Nagual typically has a surplus of life energy, it becomes consumed in these trying times. This allows a seer to focus their awareness inward, on what their real purpose is.

Bill:

It sounds like times of great sorrow are something that we all face at one point or another in our lives, whether we are seers or not. Perhaps we should all use this lesson to harness those difficult periods as a chance to focus, a time in which we withdraw ourselves, and our energy, from all that is not necessary in our lives. Hard times should serve to show us where we have lost our way, and where the excess exists in our lives, so that we can center ourselves and consolidate our efforts.

Lujan:

Well said.

NATURAL REMOTE VIEWING

Bill:

What's the difference between natural and forced remote viewing?

Lujan:

We discussed people projecting their photonic energy to other places to gain information from an area in which their awareness had arrived. I gave the example of people, during scientific experiments, demonstrating the ability to 'read' the face of a playing card in another room, or at a considerable distance. This is forced remote viewing. As I said, this quickly depletes the body's resources to perform the task and the ability is often lost shortly afterward.

Natural remote viewing is what happens when a person develops their innate capacities as a seer. Everyone has different inherent aptitudes or gifts. You can't say, "I want this ability or that." It's just not possible. You get whatever fits your configuration and that's it. That is your purpose and your life path. You just have to accept it. There is really no way to force anything without provoking consequences that may be detrimental in the end.

Natural remote viewing has to do with our third eye and our inborn ability to see. The way it works for me is that if I have someone in my presence and they're speaking to me, regardless of what they are talking about, an image will appear. It is a fleeting vision that is quite often external, but which originates with them. This phenomenon is an effect of that individual's capacity to be dimensionalized, for even though we are absorbed within this reality, it is only a holographic projection of our potential reflecting back on us. The world is a mirror. This is a very important subject, but let's stay with remote viewing for now.

When I see that particular image or holographic projection from the other person, I receive the information it has embedded in it via the fact that I recognize that it is not a feature of the living construct we are familiar with. With natural remote viewing, the image comes to you; you don't go to it. These visions are experienced as a random anomaly. They give more information in a split second than if you were to stare at a tree or mountain for six months. I can find out more about my environment with just a glimpse into those scenes than if I tried to seek out answers or insights through reading tarot cards or soliciting some form of seeing.

The key here is to understand that these scenes appear to me, or to any seer, naturally, not through manipulation. I never ask to see anything. Visions are simply presented to me as the information becomes necessary. When it comes to real seeing, you are shown what you need to witness, not what you want to see. This is where some people get off track. You can never force true information to reveal itself.

Reading tarot cards and fortune telling are examples of going out of your way to seek divine information. When you ask, "Is *this* going to happen?" or say, "The information I seek is *this* or *that*," you are attempting to bend the future to your will and your desire. This is autosuggestion in itself, whether subconscious or not. Whatever the cards 'reveal' in response to the question that has been posed will be enlaced with your original intention. Even if you understand that tarot cards or similar mediums have an essentially random basis, just as remote viewing can be understood as random, there is still an expectation lying in wait which inevitably influences the outcome.

True seeing and natural remote viewing are in essence the same thing. In most cases, you cannot select what you want to see or when you will see it. That is the difference between natural remote viewing and forced remote viewing. You must wait until the information naturally presents itself.

Bill:

You mentioned seeing information in scenes when in the presence of your students or people in general, and also projecting your photonic potential in remote viewing. Are the two events the same thing?

Lujan:

Not exactly. When you remote view, your photonic energy is cast out to a distant place. When you 'see' someone, their energy field will create the scene for you to view and gather information from. This is the difference between the two, but they are similar in the fact that you must wait in both circumstances. We wait for the information to present itself, or the visions to occur naturally. Once that content becomes available, you simply observe what has been shown.

These abilities can only be developed by living your life within the realm of your personal power and taking impeccable responsibility for yourself, not by forcing the events to take place. By willing your photonic energy out into the universe or demanding information from the world around you, you will take yourself off your life path and potentially divert your environment from its natural evolutionary course.

Bill:

Okay, let's stay with this concept of allowing your seeing to naturally occur and not attempting to leverage the world around you. Should we follow this path when dealing with dreaming? I don't attempt to go into lucid dreaming intentionally, but sometimes I wake up in a dream spontaneously. Is 'natural dreaming' the same as natural remote viewing or seeing? You have advised me to not dream at all. I guess what I want to know is: What do I do when dreaming occurs without my intending it to happen? Am I still in the same energetic danger of being hijacked by inorganic awareness if it occurs in this way?

Lujan:

You need to pay attention to what you have absorbed. When you wake up, you will have a natural influx of visual information. It will be jumbled, meaningless material unless it has a potent amount of emotional input within it. When there is emotional content, it is an indicator that a message is imminent. You receive this with your body, through the emotion, as true composites of insight that pertain to what you need to realize. If there is real information there, then you can assume that you have dreamed correctly. You learn from your dream. You receive the lesson from your own body consciousness, not from the emissary, or a voice, or some entity.

You can enter into natural dreams without interfering with the dream content, but you have to learn to recognize the contradictions that reveal themselves in comparison to who you really are, which can be hard to discern if you are not clear. The markers that reveal inorganic interference are that the content of the dream will be contrary to the life of impeccability that you are living.

When you conduct yourself with integrity, you will know when the feelings that arise are not in accordance with your true nature, and this will become self-evident by virtue of the fact that the warrior has made the choice not to live contradictions. If this is not the case, then you will be occupied with the contradictions and compromises of your daily life, in one form or another. If the dream content does not feel harmonious, you can more than likely assume that you are being interfered with.

CONFIDENCE

Bill:

The other day, you said something to me that I have been thinking about. You said that the difference between you and I is that you believe in yourself and your seeing, and that I do not.

Lujan:

That's right. You don't fully believe in yourself.

Bill:

I seem to find myself always checking for the rational answer for things around me. I see a shadow move across the room and I'm looking for a monster in the corner, when I see a moth around the light. Every time I brush against the second attention and 'see', I instantly have an explanation for it. Sometimes the information is embedded in the scene, as you have described, but at other times, my eyes are playing tricks on me and I feel like I am indulging in fantasyland.

I have met people who believe that everything they see is an omen or has some secret meaning. God forbid a crow flies by. I don't want to be this way, and I can't let go of some little part of me that makes me disbelieve in what I see, even if it's just the smallest amount. How do I get that last bit of confidence that so clearly marks our difference?

Lujan:

You either see or you don't. It's when you play into what you think you are seeing that you get in trouble, like searching for illusions to validate your position as a seer, not too dissimilar to seeing the shadow of a moth and assuming it is something other than what it really is. Genuine omens or indications are usually preceded by an ominous feeling, which alerts your body consciousness that something real is coming. In a lot of warrior's lives, this is rare unless they've gathered a certain amount of personal power.

I'll give you an example of seeing without adding one's personal interpretation. A friend of mine came to see me the other day. When I saw her approach the door, I instantly knew she would not come inside. I saw this from the combination of her body language and the energy around her being. The luminous bubble surrounding her appeared as if it had folded back on itself, making only a half, and I knew then she was not going to enter the house.

She said she did not have much time to stay, and she handed me a computer part she had brought me. While she was talking, she noticed that I was looking above her, about twelve feet up. I could actually see her energy leaving as she was intending to withdraw. You could say that was an omen. It was a clear indication of what she was about to do. I knew I couldn't invite her in, as my wife and I usually do. It was visually apparent that she was retreating, even though she was approaching. This is seeing and I had to accept it.

If I weren't seeing, I would have invited her in and she would have had to become more forceful with her body language and refuse the invitation. People who don't see would only know what the person had told them and, depending on their own emotional state, could even be offended by this refusal. On a certain level they may sense what the other person's body is saying to them, but they don't recognize it. They are too engaged in the social interaction to be conscious of what their body knows. On the level where people see the energy directly and have no choice but to acknowledge what is seen, the social element becomes irrelevant in comparison to the real exchange.

A lot of people say to me that I am a body language expert. While I do receive huge amounts of information from physical inflections, I am more adept at reading the energy around a person's body, which actually delivers me insight in terms of their true directives. Then my eyes go to their physicality. The silent reservoir of our body consciousness ultimately dictates our intentions, even before we become aware of it. If you are thirsty, your energy will move to pick up the glass of water before your body does, and then your physicality will respond accordingly. When I meet a person, I see their internal reservoir of potential first. From this, a seer can deduce what is really going to occur.

For you personally, Bill, if you want to avail yourself to these capacities, you need to get over the desire to 'see'. When a seer observes these phenomena, in a lot of cases, they really don't want to be involved at all, for what is seen leaves unnecessary impressions. When you get to that threshold, you will know exactly what I am talking about. This is what was meant when it was written that there are no volunteers in the world of power. There can be no application of personal will in terms of omens and seeing. You are subject to what is going on, whether you like it or not.

You become virtually imprisoned at certain stages due to your seeing, but you don't have the ability to command what you see. You receive it because you are open to it; not because you want it, but because you are naturally aware enough to be engaged on that subtle plane of communication. Then you are left with the choice as to whether you will verbally transmit that information to another person and help them grow to the next level of self-awareness, or not.

That is what a Nagual does; they teach others to be aware of what is presenting itself. The way you are being taught by me is that you are getting visual images inside your head when I convey my seeing to you. You had the image of my friend coming to see me, and her energy field, when I was describing that, didn't you?

Bill:

Yes.

Lujan:

Right. You see this because it is not something fictitious. It's real. I can't explain things that are not real. You can't make up a story about seeing. You have to give genuine, potent circumstances so that scene can be transmitted to the listeners – you, in this case – as living visualizations. Then you are starting to communicate. It's just like learning to read or walk or ride a bike. We have to be given something to work with.

It has also been said there is no such thing as a 'corner-store shaman'. This is true. You can't go and say, "I want a vanilla or chocolate sorcery package today." That's not possible. You can't pick and choose what path you will be put on. You get what you get. It will be what you need and what you are meant to encounter, not what you want. So if you go and summon a 'corner-store shaman' and say, "I want *this*," or "I want to know *that*," the answers they will give you will be phony, since that is not how real seeing works.

Our relationship functions on the basis of exploring what naturally arrives in the moment. If you were to turn back the years of our training and friendship, neither one of us would have guessed we would be here having this type of communication. How could we? You would have been surprised, as you are obviously surprised now, at the information you are getting, because it's not what you expected. This material you have here is the only thing that can be delivered, via the fact that there is not an expectancy system in place between us. Our communal attention, devoid of expectation, propagates the transmission of real power and insight.

As soon as you have an expectation, real seeing retreats, and as it contracts, it removes one's connection with Spirit or the universe as a whole. The most valuable thing a human can have is their connection to Spirit. If you lose that, you lose everything. This is exactly the same thing that exists between you and I. I will lose my universal connection if I try to force you to see something that is not true. When I am teaching you, I can only give you genuine examples of my seeing to help you learn.

True seeing is random, fast and fleeting, and one must have incredible speed in their life to catch sight of their own seeing. By giving you my seeing, it allows you the possibility to assimilate, on an internal visual level, information that you can then start to wait for. When you come across it in your own life, you will recognize it, for you will go back to this circumstance as a teaching tool that will interlink with the omen that you are being shown at the point your fledgling wings begin to open up. Thus you begin to see.

This is what a Nagual is supposed to do. We are meant to give you true-life situations so you can become an authentic seer, yourself. These teachings will serve as a point of reference for you to be able to say, "Okay, I just saw it, and that's what Lujan was talking about." Then when you witness the phenomena yourself, you find a reference point of your own and you go from there. You will no longer need my reference point. It will be replaced with your own experience, and the knowledge and power will reside with you.

These shared visions become our communal conductivity in terms of what I see and what you have experienced, as in the case of the woman coming to my door with the intent to leave and her energy bubble being pulled back. By communicating that image to you, I am increasing my ability to see through utilizing my capacity of transmission as it becomes available in connection with your receptivity to learn more about who you are as a luminous being.

This is exactly how the tradition of verbal transmission between shaman and apprentice has worked for millennia. It works only when the interchange is based on true experiences of power and seeing. You couldn't go to a university and learn this, because the transmission would be subject to someone who wasn't passing on real experiences. The information would be exchanged on an intellectual or theoretical basis. Theoretical does not work for the seer, as there is no real power there. Teaching has to come from a genuine experience of the seer communicating with you. You can't indirectly transmit the experiences of someone else's power.

Now, a while back you mentioned patience. Your dilemma right now is that you are not confident that your waiting has the necessary gravity to draw power to you. You don't fully trust yourself yet, as you haven't had many genuine experiences of seeing up until now. When I talk to you and give you my stories of true experiences, your confidence to patiently wait must come about from knowing that this has been an authentic transfer of information, which you know, for your body has received the visual image. This can also occur with written tales of power, but it depends on how much information is locked in them, the energy levels of the person reading them, and also on the personal power of the individual who created them.

Bill:

So it seems that I am patiently waiting for my power and seeing to evolve and present itself.

Lujan:

You can't even wait patiently. You have to wait without waiting. If you focus on waiting, you will be perpetually immobile within that intention. Your energy will be spent on the idea of expectation within the waiting, and then you will seek validation for that activity. The moment you seek validation, you will feel entitled to have something happen. As soon as you feel entitlement, you become gripped in all the undercurrents of the social conditioning that has been given to you since birth. You were formatted with this programming in order to continually validate yourself and seek recognition.

The only way to be recognized in the world of power, or as a seer, is to disappear. The only way to disappear is to not seek validation. You let the world validate itself to you. Speak to the truth of what you see and then faithfully observe what occurs from that point. At that crucial juncture you will be validating Spirit and the universe itself, and no longer attempting to validate yourself. You speak on behalf of something larger than yourself and you become a true conduit via this selfless application.

Bill:

When you talk about the abstract cores of sorcery tales, aren't you transmitting the experience of someone else's power?

Lujan:

In this case, I become aware of the information that's locked within the abstract core, and then through insight, reveal something that was absolutely hidden, as opposed to reciting the original transmission verbatim. The first method reveals truth in comparison to the power of the warrior. The second is purely repetition of what has already been established. The expounding of information in this way identifies false seers via the source material being dogmatically adhered to, thus turning wisdom into religion.

True religion is living the absolute application of wisdom, and this will never be applied in the same way twice. That is why, within the parameters of transmission, there is always great change, revealing the endless resources that adapt to the circumstance, which indicate a way to proceed that is harmonious in comparison to the power available.

REINCARNATION AS A DIMENSIONAL SHIFT

Bill:

Reincarnation is a concept I have heard people discuss all my life. It is mentioned in most religions in some form or another. What is your belief on reincarnation?

Lujan:

I don't believe anything until the moment truly arrives. I have personal experiences involving reincarnation to confirm whether it is real or not. This phenomenon is verifiable through these experiences, but the reality of how it happens does not really correspond with the understanding that everyone has been exposed to. Its cosmic application is infinitely more complex than what is socially acceptable in most theological circles.

Go back to the example of the playing card and the seer sending his photonic energy to identify the unknown playing card. They are keeping the card stable as a holographic unit of information, which they are able to access, demonstrating that they were there, seeing through structures that they normally would not be able to gain entry to. What happened to me regarding reincarnation was exactly the same kind of thing, but my experience was within dimension.

About fifteen years ago, I lived and died as a monk in Tibet, but the lifetime I visited belonged to a much earlier time, maybe one hundred and fifty years before I saw it. It was fifteen years ago that I received the realization that I was living as a monk, but when I traveled to that awareness, it had been decades since I had existed in that lifetime. _

Now, this interdimensional access, which came to me as a vision, wasn't borne of my photonic energy being connected to some entity in dreaming that was creating an illusion for me. My photonic energy was in my heart and I was asleep, and somehow the scene that I existed in for a whole lifetime as a Tibetan monk became available as a composite of information.

It's important to distinguish between a dream and a vision in a dream. Real dreaming is the point at which you reference information through a vision. This access point to my memories was a holographic scene that manifested itself in the second attention. This anomaly connected me to the first attention of a world where a human being had been living many years ago, who *was* me. Now, this probably sounds a little confusing and intertwining.

Bill:

Just a little?

Lujan:

That is just the way it is. When I was sleeping, I had the full vision that I was a monk in Tibet, and I was seeing something of the area where I lived. Upon that sight, my photonic energy raced out of my heart center and traveled with enormous speed to the space and time that I existed in all those decades ago. All of a sudden there were mountains and snowy ground in front of me. I saw what appeared to be a barn, but I didn't quite recognize the construction since I am a living Westerner at this time. I assume it was a barn of sorts.

The first impression that came upon me was, 'Why am I here? Why am I in Tibet, looking at this?' As soon as I asked that question, my photonic energy rapidly traveled again, passing through the nearest wall of the structure. I was suddenly standing before a monk who appeared to be about thirty-five. He seemed very strong and clear. He was attending to the body of an older monk who had just recently died. He was placing objects on the chakras of the dead monk's body. I realized instantly that he was doing what I used to do: Prepare the bodies of the deceased to ascend into death.

I looked at the monk and he saw me. You know when you go to the movie theater and you look at the back of someone's head, and they turn around and look you dead in the eye and you get a shock from it? This is how I felt when I realized that the monk could see me. He looked me straight in the eye. I wondered how he could see me, since this was just the projection of my photonic self. I have no idea how I must have looked to him. Maybe he saw a light or a misty-looking figure. Who knows? When he looked at me, I saw that he knew he was seeing his old friend, his teacher; the monk who had died and whose body he was attending to now. As soon as he recognized who I was, the scene ended and my awareness flew back into my chest.

As my photonic energy was speeding back to my body, I saw a cabinet. In this cabinet were my old robe and my glasses, along with a few other personal objects that were mine when I was alive as the monk. They had been put away for safe keeping by the younger monk I had just seen. These objects were kept because these monks were looking to find a child to come and claim them. Knowing that they had belonged to this being in the previous life, they would know through that child's recognition that their old teacher had returned.

My experience is not what most would define as reincarnation exactly, since it was a concurrent, alternate existence that I witnessed. Some would say that this means I have been reincarnated here and have returned to an old life. However, this is not the case, as I revisited that time continuum only fifteen years ago and I am living now. Certainly from a traditional perspective this would be interpreted as accessing memories of a past existence. However, I relay what I've seen in comparison to my true experience of dimensionalization, which I am delineating here as a bridge of sorts to awaken this awareness within you.

When it occurred, I was conscious of the time sequence and I knew that I had been living here when I died there. Even though the continuum did exist hundreds of years ago, the experiences existed simultaneously within dimension. This is possible by virtue of the fact that the cosmos spirals and leaves traces of itself within vortexes which can be opportunistically entered if the etheric fiber optics of interdimensional universal connectivity are in symbiotic alignment with the seer. To give a visual image, this is not too dissimilar to when one waves their hand very quickly in front of their face and sees trace images fanning out, showing every location occupied upon that trajectory.

Multifaceted, parallel time continuums correspond to the quantum physics principle of the 'superposition', which describes the fluid interactivity of matter on a subatomic level. Essentially what is highlighted here is that all things exist in a state of unlimited potentiality until their position is verified or observed, thus allotting them a specific space-time point of reference. This is equally reflected in the macrocosmos via the manifestation of any organized construct, and pertains to all bio-electromagnetic frequencies' amassment upon a point of arrival.

The extrapolation of this discovery, on the level of awareness, is that, if we refrain from identifying with the assumption that we know what is, we can avail ourselves, as individuals and collectively, to a much greater spectrum of possibilities.

These findings of quantum physics are quantifiable in shamanism. As long as the empty intention applied is compatibly configured to the predetermined outcome of the shaman's destiny, then the possibility for absolute transmutation is available. In simpler terms, be without being, know without knowing, and do without doing.

When one directly experiences these dimensional anomalies, only truth can be conveyed. The body will understand what is absorbed or witnessed, and the feeling will be one of irrefutable certainty that the vision and the information contained within are true. The realization I was presented with was that I was living here as well as elsewhere, interdimensionally, within a full lifetime as a Tibetan monk.

So we can say there is reincarnation, but not exactly as it has been understood. It is more accurate to think of it as a dimensional shift. Even twenty years ago, before I had this vision, I already had so much Tibetan information. I knew things that I shouldn't know, since I am not a Tibetan in this life. The life I lived as a monk was almost eighty years long, but it ended fifteen years ago, and I have lived almost sixty years in this life. So there is a crossover.

Reincarnation is understood as linear; I live here as Lujan and then I die, and then I am reborn again in a new life later on, and so on. However, it is not that clear cut. The simplest explanation for this most mysterious process has been given to placate the limited consciousness of the receiver, since most cannot yet grasp the multidimensional facets of their real self.

The reason that people do not comprehend dimensionality is that the collective frequency has been stilted due to the fact that our photonic energy is being consumed in a multiplex of engagements, in our waking world and within dreams, which insidiously overlap. Once we have been dreamed in the predator's world, in most cases, it becomes very difficult to escape our preoccupations within our waking construct. The predatorial insertion molds the unfathomable aspects of our reality into a compounded linear sequence. The waking world loops into dreams, and the dreams loop into the waking world, so that a limiting self-reflection is permanently sustained. This reflection seems to reveal the truth of our reality, but unfortunately contains our potential within stifling parameters. Our predicament is not too dissimilar to the labyrinthine illusion portrayed in the Escher paintings of stairwells.

Our capacity to go beyond the vital scope that necessitates growth of consciousness must be realized through the amassment of our true potential. We need to sincerely revise our conceptualization to encompass the full spectrum of possibilities that our multidimensionality represents. When a seer becomes totally aware of the implications of their journey then their body consciousness is alerted and thus educated for their upcoming incarnation.

I will tell you another story that will give you another perspective upon this vast subject matter. I was driving down a highway, taking my wife to the hospital for a doctor's visit, when three little birds flew out in front of the car and slammed into my windshield. I felt bad for the little birds, as I knew they had died. A second later, a large semi trailer passed by on the opposite side of the road and nothing happened. In that exact same instant, the same truck jackknifed and crashed into our car, extinguishing our life forces at that point in time.

There I was, driving to the hospital with my wife and simultaneously being killed in an alternate reality. This was once again a case of my photonic energy going to a parallel continuum that existed, just not here and now. I even saw my friends and students standing at my graveside. Instantly, I was back in this reality, driving down the road.

I immediately picked up my cell phone and called my friend, Naomi. "I just died!" I said, and she responded, wide eyes visible in the tone of her voice, "Lujan, how is it possible for you to call me from the other side?!"

I almost cried, I was laughing so hard, but her innocence was so moving. I described my experience in the alternate reality and how she and everyone else were grieving me. I told her how in that life, they had to continue their lives without me, but in this life, I get to continue with them. The fact of the matter is that there *are* multiple realities. We can only experience these things, and there may never be exact answers that provide the types of explanations that most people want to hear. You're going to have to get used to this.

I have another example for you. I was driving again, but I don't remember where this time. Suddenly my awareness was transported to a scene in some other country. I was standing outside of a church, looking around. About the time I realized where I was, I returned to my awareness here, driving down the road. I looked up and there was a car coming to a stop in front of me. I slammed on the brakes and stopped just in time.

Bill:

Remind me to drive next time we go anywhere!

Lujan:

(Laughing.) I don't know what's up with me and cars, but I do seem to project myself a lot while driving and I am totally unconscious when I do.

Bill:

Fabulous!

Lujan:

Two years ago, when I was in Jamaica with my wife, I had another experience of non-linear time. I was looking into her eyes and she turned into an ebony-skinned, luminous being that was emerging directly from the source. She had strange tattoos that looked like black arrows going down the center of her body. Her eyes were big and dark and she had a very small nose and mouth. As she came through, she was so beautiful and magnificent, and I knew that she had entered into this reality at that very moment.

As she looked at me, she saw me as a similar dark-skinned being coming from the void-like state, finally meeting and conjoining in that moment. The message she had for me was that she was here to fulfill all that I was not, and that she had never been born before. When I saw her, we simultaneously realized that we both came from our point of origin. At that time, she had been alive for about forty years and for me it had been over fifty.

My wife's parents have the memory of her being born, and she has the memory of her childhood. My family has the memory of me being born, and I have the memory of my childhood. But those timelines are illusions. We only just appeared at that particular moment. Our whole story, the beginning and the end, were created to justify our presence here, and thus we become lost to the fact that we just arrived.

The rules of this holographic construct say you have to be born and you have to live, you can't just come here and exist. And just like that, you forget where you are coming from. You become consumed with the story of your beginning and your end, and the linear process you are confronted with. To wake up to the reality of what has just been described, Bill, is so very difficult.

Now, the truth of what I am revealing is also coming from the source, and this explanation will enable you to understand our experience of the holographic universe, which is our lifetimes coexisting. This reality is only one example of the multiplex. If we pop out of this original source point in multidimensional positions, you know what's going to happen?

Bill:

I have no idea.

Lujan:

Multidimensional universes, where we simultaneously are born, exist and die. You see, the source point is not subject to time. At this moment, we are in the process of becoming totally aware that we are subject to an avalanche of existences, which, in fact, really do not exist. This timeless emptiness has been masked by the fact that our source point appears not to be the origin of every single moment that we have existed in since the beginning of the universe, for we are so linearly fixated. Yet the beginning and end of the universe are only understandings, borne of the fact that we have forgotten that we have only just appeared.

Something else I realized when my wife and I experienced the source point is that this state is filled with so much compassion, love, peace, and understanding. It is composed of everything that we struggle to bring into our existence as human beings; to fully love, to completely understand, to be nonviolent, and to exist within harmony. When we are in our buoyant, void-like existence, we understand all of these things. But when we come to this reality, we must struggle to retain and remember the purity of our beginning.

Bill:

What exactly do you mean by 'source point'?

Lujan:

Physicists know that all molecules and atoms that make up the world are held in place by something, but they don't really have a name for it. It is 'source point'. They can tell you that there is a table in front of you, but when you go all the way down to the smallest particles, there is always space in between, which binds all things. What is holding it together is the source, and what creates the illusion of linear continuity and solid matter is our collective fixation upon duality.

What you have to understand is that when my wife and I appeared here in this construct, it was only two years ago. If I have done it, then you have done it and so has everyone else, but we all suffer from the interlocking aspect of the construct, demanding that our awareness conform to the rules and regulations that are the constraining parameters of this reality, or this attention.

Bill:

I have to admit that I am not really following what you are trying to convey here. Quite frankly, I am totally confused.

Lujan:

Okay. I see that you are lost because you don't have a reference point for the information. You don't have a personal experience with which to parallel what I'm explaining. What you are having difficulty comprehending is that we arrived in this life *at that moment*, even though when it occurred I was in my fifties and she was in her forties. It is very difficult to describe how the living construct reproduces the reality that generates the memories of present, past and future simultaneously. What I am now realizing is that I have to define this in a way that you and other people experience it.

If you look at what I just explained from a linear perspective – which is how most people will – what I experienced is what you will undergo at the end of your life. When humans die, they are presented with their entire lifetime and all of their pertinent doings at the moment of departure. They are delivered into a position in which they can review their journey in that final instant.

The difference between this 'normal' situation and what I experienced is that my wife and I were presented with our entire life sequence – past, present and future – in the middle of our lives. As strange as it sounds, it was clear to us that this was the point at which we arrived here into this world.

Another difference is that we were not shown all the visual imagery of our lives, like someone normally is at death. We were simply presented with the realization of what we were meant to do in this existence.

The multidimensional aspect of this reality is a very difficult concept to comprehend. I have given many illustrations of this, here and in my other books. One case is my story of the Tibetan monk. I lived and died as that monk, while I existed in this reality as myself. This is the true nature of our existence that I am endeavoring to convey to you, Bill. Time is not as linear as most would like to think.

I know the vastness of this information is hard to assimilate at the moment, but you will come to terms with these things through your own experiences eventually. I am just an initial catalyst to open you up to the inevitability of your own journey, which will become the stories that you will transmit to another.

Another illustration I can give you is the story of how I became a Nagual, which I spoke of in my first book. I was seven years old when I was first confronted by the whispering aspect of the shadow's attention, which was directing my mother's awareness away from her true sovereignty. It spotted me seeing it and it raced at me. At this point, I have the memory of the old Nagual Lujan intervening on my behalf. He lived several hundred years ago, yet entered into my time continuum just a few decades ago.

Via this contact, I have inherited all of his most potent memories. The old Nagual passed through time and space to continue in me. I am not totally him, but I am not the same person that existed before the intervention either. We are a new being, a combination of our awarenesses.

I hope that my explanations about this phenomenon are sufficient enough to bring you to a point of resolution, thus preparing your body consciousness into a natural state of reception for these eventualities.

It doesn't matter how much you know in this life, nor is it a requirement to know anything. All that counts is that you know how to wait, and how to act in a circumstance as it confronts you by the pressure it applies. This is the only secret that has any value. All of the experiences I have had are not of great consequence; the only thing that has meaning is how I conduct myself. We have to believe in this.

This is like faith, but it is not faith. It is more than faith. It is waiting to see what you are meant to do. You can only see what you are meant to do at the point that it reveals itself. In between, you have to wait. The waiting is not faith, either. Waiting reveals the silent determination of the warrior in terms of their non-insistence upon an outcome.

The way in which we patiently bide our time gives gravity and potency to our attention. If we wait with expectation, our attention will not have the power to allow the true elusive moment to appear, which can't be solicited. Our multidimensional nature's influx upon our attention is indefinable. Waiting is where our true fortitude comes into play.

Bill:

I understand.

LIGHT FILAMENTS

Bill:

I have some questions about your benefactor, the old Nagual Lujan. You said that this man lived several hundred years ago.

Lujan:

That's correct. He came to me when I was seven years old and again when I was forty. He removed one of my energy compartments and returned it thirty-three years later, as this was the only possible way for him to interact with me.

Bill:

Were you aware of him at the age of seven?

Lujan:

Yes.

Bill:

Did all of your Nagual information come to you at the age of forty when he returned your energy compartment?

Lujan:

No. The information has always been there. There was a culmination point, though, at the moment I saw his suit of armor flying through the air, possessing all of his experiences. When I gazed into his mask, there was nothing behind it; only the void filled his armor.

Throughout my life, I would see him or his armor following me. Sometimes he was an ancient Asian man with long, gray hair. There were many experiences that I haven't yet written about. He would take me and show me things about our planet and the filaments of light that surround the earth. He taught me how to clear the filaments of objects that look like beetles, actually.

Bill:

What were these beetles?

Lujan:

I'm not totally sure. They looked like insects, plugging up the filaments of light that are surrounding the planet. He was directing me to clear those.

Bill:

Did these beetles have to do with any one person in particular or a place or an event?

Lujan:

No. No information about what they were or why we were clearing them was transmitted. All I knew was that they were clogging the light filaments and we had to clear them. In fact, they weren't clogging the filaments as much as they were bending them and when I brought my awareness to the fact they were there, they were cleared. What a strange concept, to be directed to do something and you do nothing but become aware of it, and the change is made.

Bill:

I don't actually find that strange at all. That's how we're supposed to remove our negative social programming, is it not? We gently focus on it without self-judgment. We bear witness without attachment.

Lujan:

(*Laughing.*) Yes, that is a very clear way to look at it.

THE ROUND SHADOW

Lujan:

Lately there has been a lot of social drama in the village that I live in. This led to a very interesting event that occurred the other night while I slept.

Bill:

Do tell?

Lujan:

I mentioned to you that when we appear in this construct, we arrive through the dark matter. Upon that emergence, we must take a form, as does every entity, whether organic or inorganic. Certain shapes determine awareness, and some are very ancient.

The other night as I slept, I became awakened to the fact that I was standing outside of my home. My awareness was within the projection of my photonic eye and as I scanned my environment, I saw that I was in the courtyard between the other buildings. The night was clear and crisp, with no wind. Looking up, I realized that I was in front of a dark, spherical entity, several meters in diameter. It appeared as a big, round shadow. I knew instantly that this being was very old and I knew why it was here.

The dark mass emanated a strong magnetic pull to draw on my photonic energy, a source of fuel for this being. These particular entities are engaged in tracking and hunting that resource which is our energy, and the round shadows do this by entering our construct. In order to stalk our photonic potential, they have to somehow get involved in our reality. The way they accomplish this is to take possession of an individual's dream reality during their nighttime visitations to our first attention ream.

The round shadow connects us to their magnetic field through engaging our self-limiting perceptions, which creates a direct feed line from our photonic reserve into their energetic matrix. They don't bargain; they just take our awareness and replace it with theirs. Once this is established, their mind becomes ours. This is how seers can get caught, and is precisely why one shouldn't go into dreaming without firstly clearing imprinted awareness, in order to have the ability to actualize some form of clear-sightedness within that domain.

The entity was able to appear here due to the fact that there was a lot of social drama being played out in the village, involving quite a few people. I became interested in what was going on when I discovered that the energy in the area was being blocked. I began to focus on this and that is when this thing appeared, at around 2 or 3 o'clock in the morning of the same night. When I looked into this dark mass of awareness, I received a surge of information on the local drama flooding in all at once.

You see, the daytime world of the people continues to whisper at night, and through that vibrational gateway, these shadows slip in. The fact is that everything we say and do gets absorbed by the environment we are living in. The trees, plants, animals, and buildings, all soak up the feelings of our reality. When our social content is projected into the night while we sleep, these entities pass through upon that resonance and further inflame the social situations and dramas that enthrall us within the first attention.

They accomplish this by luring our awareness off into dreams that make no sense, magnifying and distorting the memories that we possess, and catering extensively to the dreamer. Most people don't even notice this elusive drain because they have no concern for seeing or for our true dimensional nature, and are unfortunately fully engaged by the grind of their mundane lives. Meanwhile, shadow beings are working behind the scenes, using all of that energy and drama to create dream positioning that waylays the photonic energy of the individuals involved.

Bill:

So these shadow-like beings are living off the photonic energy that is being wasted by people in their dramatic social behavior?

Lujan:

Its potential to get here relies on the fact that the energetic resonance of their drama, which isn't in accordance with their life path, provides the portal through which the shadow can appear and function within our realm. Once you are centered in your personal power, these beings won't have access to you, since your photonic energy will not be randomly flung out into the universe anymore.

This is what is meant by a 'broken gourd' or 'cracked vessel'. You can pour as much water as you like into a cracked gourd and everything that goes in will leak out. It doesn't matter how much information you give someone if their energy is being siphoned into alternate realms via these entities, or through that individual going into dreaming intentionally, their vital resources will be wasted. There comes a point where there is no way to retrieve them energetically and they may never fully develop on their path as a seer.

There are many popular sorcery stories of people being saturated in dreaming to the point that they become lost in that world. One particular story was relayed about seers going into the realm of inorganic beings to retrieve individuals trapped there. Unfortunately, once a part of someone is fully engaged in that fixation, it is almost impossible to seal the crack this creates in their energy field. Their photonic reserves will leak into the dream realm as long as that contact is maintained.

Bill:

How do we deal with these things? Is there some way to fight back or to shrug them off?

Lujan:

You combat these things through understanding. You don't fight them physically or go into their world and have a battle with them. Your battle of power is in you willing yourself not to be involved. The answer lies in the internal dialogue. You must endeavor to turn it off, but most people don't seem to have the ability to do that as they are divided within. The only voice that belongs to us is that of the heart that speaks and realizes. The rational mind should only be used for counting and measuring things, little more.

Bill:

How is our photonic energy consumed?

Lujan:

We share our photonic potential through interaction. It is used to create the construct that confronts you. While you're viewing that dream scene, it may appear that you are in control, but the scene itself is absorbing your energy. Everybody is familiar with the point where a dream just ends. That is when you are out of photonic energy. A certain potential has gone into sustaining the dream and then it's over.

It's like when you are aware that you must leave. You just know. Your energy knows it is being drained and you realize it is time to go. At the point when you drop out of the dream, the inorganics have absorbed the maximum amount of your photonic potential that they can.

Bill:

Is it like being tired?

Lujan:

No, it's not like being tired. It's like when you are talking to someone and the conversation just comes to an end as you know it can't go any further, so then a person gets up and leaves. Same principle.

In dreaming it is not possible to go on and on and become exhausted, for the rules are absolute. When the dreamer reaches a certain threshold, they simply return. The reason you are having difficulty understanding this is that we are socially bound to be polite and we quite often overstay our welcome, which in turn does drain our energy extensively.

This is the only reality where you can get away with that kind of behavior. The cause of this condition is a dualistic compromise that is taking place internally. This incongruency feeds into the predator's agenda by weakening our integrity so that our actions, words, and imaginations will be sent into the ether at dusk, to be whispered back to us through dream scenes that waste our time just as much as we've wasted it ourselves.

Bill:

So what you are saying is that people should move more with their intuition or heart, and less with the pre-programmed mind, for in that context lurks the internal dialogue and the gate to the shadow?

Lujan:

Exactly.

DIFFERENT TYPES OF SEEING

Bill:

In the conversations we have had, you have described 'seeing' in different manners. One is by observing a holographic scene appear outside of your mind, in which there is information embedded that you are instantly aware of. You also describe seeing things like the energy bubble around a person, or witnessing your Double, or the light fields of the world. I have experienced the 'scene' type of seeing. Seeing for me seems more like a knowing.

Sometimes I will suddenly have an insight into something or someone. It feels like when you have been working on a long math problem or something that has been confusing you and then, suddenly, you understand the equation and the information floods in. Is what I experience seeing?

Lujan:

Everybody has a different capacity for seeing.

Bill:

Does one type of seeing lead to the next?

Lujan:

Not necessarily. All of the types of seeing you have just described, I have experienced in various ways. Everyone experiences exactly what you are speaking of, but do they remember? Do they have the energetic capacity to realize what they are aware of?

Our awareness of the predator also works like this, in that we have the capacity to perceive it, but we struggle to retain the consciousness of what we notice. A lot of people will see the predator when they are children, dwelling in the ether outside of their body, and in dreams and nightmares. They become so frightened that they fearfully internalize themselves from that point onwards, instead of opening their eyes to the possibilities they are naturally aware of.

As children, we naturally see through our photonic eye as well as through our physical eyes, since our heart is functioning clearly. Later on, the child will see those extraneous scenes or holographic images that are so terrifying and, when their parents tell them that it's their imagination, they lock this in their heart and lose the desire and ability to see within dimension. It is the visceral dread of witnessing something sucking on their life force that drives children to fortify their awareness within the first attention, for the social eddy is so strong that they find refuge in it, and that solace is a trap. This is how seeing is initially suppressed. That magical potential is then diverted into social fixations, which in turn translate into self-reflective dream imagery.

Once seeing becomes internalized, the predator starts to integrate by coercively whispering to conjure that imagery. This is the beginning of the internal dialogue, and the young seer is left in a quandary. There is now an installed voice that determines the social dictums of their behavior and they lose access to their true voice, which remains that of an undeveloped child as a result.

Retrieval as an adult is truly a difficult process, for when this voice emerges it is so undefined, relative to that false internal reflection which they have become accustomed to. It's so subtle in comparison to the brashness of the attention that is right in front of us our whole lives. All of the experiences you have spoken about in reference to seeing are valid and you will continue to be subjected to them all.

Bill:

You mentioned seeing the filaments of light around the planet and I have read other similar accounts. I have never seen such a thing. Will I? If I continue to break my social programming, will I eventually develop to that point or is this an all-or-nothing situation? I don't see it now, so I never will?

Lujan:

I can't determine that for you, Bill, but that is why it is so important for us to be a human collective of seers, not just a group of ten, twelve, or sixteen seers as has been portrayed in some sorcery writings. It's essential that we begin to realize and accept that we all have different capacities, which eventually will be congruently combined so that we see as one.

We all really do see in the ways described here, we just have trouble remembering. We just don't recognize it, or don't want to acknowledge it, or have difficulty summoning the energy to put the pieces of the puzzle together. I don't know which one it is for you, but clearly you aren't fully conscious of what you are capable of.

There are also points in the day in which I won't see the energy bubble around a person, or the connective strands of light, or perceive someone's intentions, for I was not meant to see that at that time. I see what I am directed to see and what presents itself to me. Indications from Spirit can equally arrive as a verbal cue or a physical gesture, or an image of someone, internally or externally realized.

What I mean by this is that the omen may present itself as a holographic – i.e., visual – unit of information, or it may manifest externally as something like a loud sound from the environment that alerts me with its poignant timing to pay particular attention to what is happening. This can be likened to a heightened form of intuition, which is not accompanied by vacillation or doubt, though it is often mysterious until the full process unfolds in due time. Sometimes I am working with all of these elements at once. So if I am stripped of the capacity to see the filaments of light, for example, then I receive something else.

The question is: Do we have the speed of perception to actually remember these moments? That is the real issue here. One of the hardest things to retain is seeing the world energetically. It is so difficult to recall, for it manifests right at source point. We usually witness these memories about twenty-four hours after the event, so then it becomes even more confusing for people. They begin to lose track of what they've seen since they are so consumed with where their attention has been relegated within the social construct.

The responsibility that we carry within ourselves as luminous beings is so vast and complex that we simply forget this very elusive factor, since, for the most part, we are energetically lagging in terms having the perceptual speed to assimilate the full scope of our interdimensional capacities.

To remember that we are actually luminous points of light and that everything around us is filled with vibrancy, yet simultaneously retains form, is one of the most difficult things to realize.

Keep in mind that when you first see this, you don't have any reference points for such things and you will usually only recall it after the event. We receive important information retrospectively, and this can be hard for people to catch onto, for they are not in the same space and time as when it happened, and may not have enough energy to assimilate unfamiliar content. Your seeing, Bill, will depend on your capacity to formulate true understandings about your place and responsibility in this part of the universe.

THE WORLD AS A MIRROR

Bill:

You once told me the world acts as a mirror, reflecting our potential back at us. What did you mean by that?

Lujan:

The world is a mirror in that it reflects to us who we are. However, if you embrace this principle too literally, it can trap you in a syntactical elitism that does not take into account the full implications of the layered, reflexive interplay that occurs within our circumstances. No matter where you go, you always arrive exactly where you are. You can travel clear across the planet, but you can never escape yourself. This is one way to look at the world as a mirror.

When you view something, it is automatically going to reflect back to you how you feel. This is truly our dilemma, for in order to evolve beyond our current position we need to inherently trust our perceptions. Hence the potential danger if this concept is interpreted without the full cognitive skills that a seer eventually arrives upon. Although this prospect may seem daunting and perhaps unobtainable, it is simply a fact that we all must grow gradually into the seat of our own personal power via the circumstances that confront us. Wisdom takes time to appear. Our personal journey will show us how we are absolutely interconnected, but will we be capable of recognizing the underlying factors at play?

One way to awaken to this reflective interconnectivity is to take into consideration what comes towards you through the vehicle of other people's intentions and actions. Be aware of the positive, but don't overlook the interplay of predatorial agendas being enacted within your environment. Until you have the relaxed detachment to be connected to the subtle factors that are unavailable to the socialized mind, which is perpetually responding via its programming, your only recourse is to wait patiently and genuinely apply yourself.

Be assured that through the eventuation of your life you will grow into this elusive sensitivity, which will allow you to see beyond the façade and connect to a greater expansion of your consciousness. In the meantime, don't allow the process of waiting to affect your lightheartedness or cloud your genuine sobriety. Let your body discover what arrives within your field of awareness and do what you have to do to arrive at the momentary truth that confronts you, without affixing paranoia to your perception.

Obviously this is a vast subject and not as simple as it initially sounds. Let me now tell you a story that will give you a better idea of how this mirroring effect functions, so that you will be able to comprehend the 'smoke' aspect, as in the concept of 'smoke and mirrors'. The factors outlined in this account will not apply to every situation, but this is something that really happened, as a clear example of the complexity we may encounter.

When I was around twenty years old, while in contact with some people from Thailand, I had a very informative encounter with a demon that originates from Southeast Asia. They were trying to manipulate me to do something that was extremely wrong, and I refused. They saw my softness as vulnerability and my innocence as something that could be controlled. In this period of my life, I did not speak very much. When I finally stated that I wanted nothing to do with their nefarious activities, a gun was pulled on me and I was warned never to say anything about what they were planning.

In the weeks following this event, I experienced very strong interference from an entity connected specifically to one individual whose influence had permeated the whole group. At this stage, I was deeply involved in hours and hours of meditation per day. When I was quietly in a space of no time, no thoughts, and no feelings, that entity, which could only be described as a demon, came into my field and presented me with a scene to view which visually revealed the strategy that was attempting to engulf the sobriety of the circumstances.

When the demon entered into my space-time continuum, it made itself apparent through an auditory presence that identified its origins, which sounded exactly like a violent wind rushing through venetian blinds. Once the sonic phenomenon manifested, the visual scene of the entity came into view. It was very tall, around about sixteen feet, and extremely muscular, with black skin that was scaly like a fish, and large demonic hands with red fingernails. To this day, it is very difficult for me to even visualize the entity's face. When the demon presented its own personal formula to my attention to manipulate me away from my center, I completely lost consciousness.

On one occasion during that time period, I found myself lying on my side on the floor, still in full lotus but several feet from where I had been sitting in the center of my bed, which was raised one-and-a-half feet off the ground. Upon finding myself unconscious twice, it became absolutely apparent how dangerous the influence of this entity was. How I dealt with these unwelcome visitations was to simply refuse any entry from this demon by willing it to have no access to my being.

Around thirty years after that experience, I was contacted by a student who was having a lot of bad luck and was being pursued by many different types of entities. He asked for my assistance and I advised him to undertake courses with me to strengthen his energy field. One afternoon, after about seven weeks of contact over a one-year period, I was demonstrating a movement from Whispering Palms, a very powerful martial form. As I walked in the interweaving circles of temple Bagua, a sound appeared right above his head. It was the exact same phenomenon that the demonic entity had manifested when it attempted to infiltrate my circumstances many years before.

The student looked at me, shocked. "What's that sound?" he asked, scanning the ceiling for its source. "There must be a big moth inside your fan."

"No, that's not it. The power that was produced from the movements I just demonstrated has revealed something hidden in your energy field."

Alarmed, he stood up and went to investigate where the sound seemed to originate. As he moved forward, the anomaly appeared behind him, coming from the glass partition, which obviously was transparent and did not reveal the large moth he was searching for. When he returned to sit down, I said to him, "You cannot control what is happening. It is probably the strongest indication that has manifested while you've been in my presence."

"This can't be possible," he exclaimed, "I've never experienced this before in my life." With these words, the sound relocated to the palm leaves of a very large tree outside.

As I watched, I saw the neighbors looking up, startled by the noise and wondering what was causing the commotion. We sat in silence and I observed his bewilderment. The sound then manifested in the kitchen, coming from the floor. In all the areas that it appeared, it would not have been possible for a large moth to get past us and remain unseen. Also, all the doors were closed; any living creature would have had to go through glass to get back inside.

It was then, on this last day of three weeks of training, that he started explaining the heavy feelings he had been experiencing before coming to see me. I began to discuss with him the maladies that were affecting him and told him that this was a very magical occurrence, for the Bagua movements had uncovered that which was hidden and needed to be revealed.

While we were speaking about everything that had transpired, I felt something plucking at my heart threads. As this disturbing feeling increased, I looked towards him, knowing that what was manifesting was trying to integrate within my emotions. But the unsettling, morose sensations arriving in my chest were not my feelings. Gazing upon him, I saw a translucent movement around his chest and neck region, viciously circling.

Knowing these projections were foreign, I whispered to myself, "This is not mine," and as I did so, black, scaly forearms appeared. Large demonic hands with red fingernails were violently gesturing around where I had previously seen the translucent activity.

I warned him immediately, "You have picked up an entity and it will make people feel aggressive towards you, increasing your own feelings of victimization. This inorganic being is very dangerous."

As soon as I finished my sentence, he told me that a friend of his had seen these very hands clearly appearing in front of her eyes. Deeply troubled, he asked, "How can I get rid of it?"

I told him he must apply an adaptation of 'Eternity's Gaze', which is a star gazing technique introduced in 'Awakening the Third Eye', where the practitioner makes a star disappear so as to dissolve unnecessary attachments to their primal being. In his case, he would need to make the star disappear three times in succession, three nights in a row. In doing so, this entity would be sent to another region of the universe.

Fortunately for my student, the previous experience that I had with this demon gave me volumes of information. Strangely enough, the rule that applies is that in making itself available, the entity reveals its modus operandi, thereby exposing the tactics being applied in connection with the person that has been possessed.

As an intermediary, I am obligated to communicate what has been discovered, even though, unfortunately, in the beginning, this is not really to anyone's advantage, for it will provoke the demon to inflame the emotional attachments that have been cultivated, which in turn are projected outwardly by the affected individual. Despite the hazardous effects that will manifest, revealing the hidden placement is absolutely necessary to solicit the growth needed to go beyond the far-reaching entrapments engendered by this antibiosis.

The afflicted individual must take full responsibility for the personal upheavals that arise, for the tactic of the demon is to enliven limiting emotions through the vehicle of self-importance. If that person does not directly address this insidious element, the entity will apply itself to drawing out this inadequacy. Then, through relentlessly engaging their surroundings in seemingly endless and insoluble dramas, that individual will enact the strategies of the entity and attempt to solicit moral support that will ultimately stifle the resolve necessary to overcome their own entrapment.

It is very common that feelings of inadequacy, worthlessness, and being misunderstood will be projected to readjust the circumstances so as to hold stable the original afflictions, which polymorphically switch into self-righteousness. These surreptitious underpinnings have pure poison at their root, as they serve to mask the possessed within their own personal pursuits to succeed, control, or dominate at all costs, even to the detriment of loved ones. The occupying demon will play into all emotional dysfunction in an attempt to nullify the awakening process, specifically focusing the myriad manifestations of the possessed individual's projected emotions upon the one who has identified its presence. This is why it is so difficult to dislodge this placement, as is the case with all inorganic attachments.

These encounters gave me the capacity to see how this entity embeds within a person's energy field. Susceptible individuals have a distinctive bone structure and head shape that indicates the aspect of their nature that can be used as an entry point. One noticeable character trait that defines these people, whether male or female, is that they desperately seek recognition through undermining the truth of their circumstances so as to create conditions whereby they can position themselves to be dominant, by applying a complex form of elitism.

Most potential leaders are targeted by this demon, for within their energetic configuration, they represent the potential to go beyond possession altogether. If they succumb to this influence, they will be collectively supported by a cartel of corrupt intent. In the case of world leaders, if they are determined and stand by their truth, resisting this infiltration, they run the significant risk of being assassinated.

The minor explanations given here are not really deep enough to elucidate the full ramifications of the parasite that affixes itself to a predisposed attention, thereby traveling into our world to wreak havoc not only in that individual's personal life but in all the circumstances it touches. Nevertheless, it is the only description I can provide at the moment.

Despite the seriousness of such a condition, those who have been possessed can easily dislodge such influences by recognizing the negative characteristics within their own behavioral patterns that need to be dissolved, thus severing the connective link. In all cases of this nature, the situation can be rectified simply through becoming of true service and acting with integrity.

As you can see, the concept of the world as a mirror is not as clear-cut as one might think. We are at a very complex crossroads of our evolution. I can only say that this experience necessitated an explanation here, not to create paranoia but to provide a description that will establish a true understanding of the multilayered position we find ourselves in. Be aware that everything is not what it seems. It is so very important to embrace non-violence so that the influence of any intention, whether socially propelled or originating from an inorganic source, has no power to enact its machinations through the vehicle of our innocence.

From this story you can observe that omens from the environment are what directed my discovery of what was at play. Such indications are reflections of the world. The question is: Are we lucid enough to see them? Omens are a form of déjà vu, which directs our lives. Either we become aware of the signs in retrospect, which is the moment at which you arrive at the event, or we see them at the intervening point of eternity. This is where the world becomes a true reflective mirror within its multiple applications to our awareness as human beings and absolutely indicates what is waiting to confront us.

If nothing untoward is happening we are usually at peace and our body will find comfort within the circumstance. Indications normally have to do with something we need to become aware of, but even when this information makes itself available, what then? Most of the time, we really can't do anything except recognize that our journey is at hand and just deal with what comes. Sometimes we can step out of the way; sometimes, we can't.

There are many disheartening influences that a seer begins to become aware of, but it is not especially beneficial for the initiate to become overly involved in negative identification, for it evokes dualism within opposition. This standpoint tends to play into predatorial agendas, whether they be organically or inorganically based.

The only value that can be found in terms of transmission of this information is that it will enable the initiate to witness human behavior, so as to comprehend through the art of stalking, the perceptual maelstroms that may confront us via the predicament that we find ourselves within. These lessons are absorbed by following the dictums of spirit and being of service to one's circumstances, so that the real world begins to unfold, thus availing the warrior to all the subtle nuances that confront us in the moment that we give ourselves completely to.

The stories that have been relayed here are but a momentary platform, to give genuine examples of our interdimensional capabilities as humans. It is for this reason that I share my experiences with you. The fact that most of us do not readily have access to our inherent capacities is a direct result of the prevailing influence of predatorial awareness. In order to access our full potential, it is so important for us to become aware of the constraints imposed upon us and how these are kept in place.

When I wrote of these matters in my first book, I felt that the descriptions given there were sufficient, but, now that I am older, I realize that these subjects need to be more deeply understood to break the spell that is upon us. Our predicament has to be elucidated from another perspective, as our capacity to be interdimensionalized is now right at our fingertips and we must take this opportunity to realize the expansive potential of our nature.

We need to allow ourselves to utilize our luminous potential to create a utopian reality, instead of pursing the haphazard path of the consumer mindset that has become inflamed over the last two hundred years and which has separated us from our precious connectivity with the energetic matrix of the planet. Remember, our dimensional capacity will manifest appropriately in comparison to any circumstance, as long as the warrior realizes that power cannot be possessed and was never theirs in the first place.

Through gathering that photonic energy which has been dispersed over the centuries, we incrementally reclaim the potential that will allow our Double to approach, and this in turn will open up interdimensional portals to our universal, central matrix.

I can't tell you why this happens when the Double gets within ten, fifteen feet of our body, it just does. The proximity of the Double avails us to our third eye potential. When we live within our integrity, we develop the fortitude to sustain the presence of the Double, and thus we become fourth-dimensionally realigned. We regain access to the forgotten aspects of our true nature, which extends far beyond the stilted format that we have been programmed into accepting.

The curbing of this precious potential is a reflection of the capacity of a predatorial awareness to influence our perception, in terms of manipulating how we see the holographic world that displays itself in front of us. This diminished view gives us the belief that we are succeeding when, in actuality, we are flailing, for we no longer even recognize ourselves within another.

Bill:

That is some deep shit.

COMMUNICATION

(Lujan and I had been discussing other subjects when this conversation started.)

Lujan:

Bill, do you have any more questions for me today?

Bill:

I did, but you covered it. As you were speaking just now, I was listening to you while blankly staring at my notes. My eyes were absent-mindedly focused on a word on the page, 'waiting'. As I was listening, your lecture drifted to the subject of waiting. You answered all of my questions without me ever actually asking you anything. How bizarre!

Lujan:

Not bizarre at all, natural. This is how communication should occur. You focused on what you wanted to ask and I spoke about what you wanted to know. This is the way we are meant to function as human beings. You don't need an internal dialogue to script a question that invites answers. All you have to do is silently focus on the information you want. If anyone in the room has anything pertinent to say, they will just talk about it. It will be their voice and their information, but your inquiry, as you and I have just experienced. This is one of the magical ways in which we operate. We all have the capability to come to each other's needs in this manner. What we must know and trust is that the most pertinent information will be delivered to us at the appropriate time.

Here is the proof of what I am saying. I didn't know that you were looking at the word 'waiting' on a piece of paper, and now we are talking about the full implications of these potent subjects. When we speak the words that are unspoken by another person, their attention and interest gives us the ability to express that information. This is what will naturally occur, as long as you have the energetic capacity to deliver the answer to the person who focused on the question to begin with. If you have enough personal power and know how to be patient, the question you don't ask will be delivered to you in a timely fashion. You just have to wait.

Bill:

Waiting without waiting?

Lujan:

Exactly.

You have to wait without waiting and not hurry toward the destination of what you want to find out or understand. The answer will be delivered to you in a fashion that is in accordance with your own personal power and your ability to assimilate the information, then in time you will have the capacity to act on it or to communicate about it to someone else.

Look at nature; it wants for nothing yet receives everything that it needs. It's the illusion that we have to achieve something that keeps us from achieving anything at all. It is upon our life path, as we strive for what we want, that we learn things we never would have thought we would learn and we become a person that we never thought we would become. We arrive at a point where we look back over our lives and say, "I couldn't have imagined it would be like this."

You end up somewhere you hadn't the slightest concept of, for you had no way of knowing where you would emerge. Yet you are still faced with the same dilemma. You want to know where you will arrive next, and you can't really determine that, even though you may focus on what you want and what you need in terms of your current ability to understand this factor. Then you get what you need, not what you wanted. This delivers you to the real essence of your humanity, which is just being patient enough to realize that everything can be known in comparison to who you are and who you are meant to be. This is why it is so important that multiple-human conductivity occurs, so that we can enrich each other with the awareness that all of us are a vital piece of the puzzle. At the moment, we are not acting as that vital piece.

Bill:

What is multiple-human conductivity?

Lujan:

It's where everybody flows from the heart and speaks what needs to be spoken at the moment it needs to be said. We live our truth through our momentary realizations, which causes a necessary ripple in the matrix that will lead to a beneficial outcome for all.

STALKING

Bill:

I have some questions about 'seeing' and 'seers' in general. What is it that ultimately makes a person a seer? You said that all people see, but that it is truly a question of remembering what we saw. Is it the cleaning up of our lives or the removing of social programming that opens us up to seeing? Is it a result of saving up enough energy to remember what we see? Is there a basic formula we can follow?

Lujan:

First, you need to stop thinking so much, and second, you need to stop doing whatever it is you have been doing all your life. If you are not succeeding as a seer, then you know whatever you have been doing is not correct for your life path. You see more than you know. I have noticed that my students are all beginning to see, since they are not participating in the social construct as they once did.

When you are sitting very quietly, you start to be ultra sensitive to what's going on in your environment. Thus you automatically deflect the insidious programming that surrounds us all by becoming aware of it.

If you can see and you use that ability to stalk your circumstances, then you are basically just a social person, maneuvering within the social world, without knowing what you are waiting for or what you are supposed to see. As a result of your projected expectations, you will decide what you wish to extract from your perception, thus distorting the true essence of your living circumstance.

Stalking as a means to personal power has been loosely interpreted as an excuse to be covertly manipulative and to feel that this surreptitiousness gives you an edge over others. Indeed, stalking is a very difficult art to come to terms with, for in reality, you can't apply yourself to it. This art inevitably has to apply itself to you. You have to wait for present pressure to gain such gravity that a cascade of previous events comes upon you, thus revealing the subtle nuances of where you have been led; which in turn retrospectively enlightens you to what has been applied to your life path. This entire book is about stalking, but it is not outwardly obvious.

Bill:

I have come to an understanding of stalking lately and it has nothing to do with what the other shamanic works have discussed. I stalk by constantly observing my environment, not by manipulating my circumstances. By quietly observing my surroundings, I know where to place myself. I am either in front of or out of the way of whatever is coming at me.

The old description of stalking seemed to be one of manipulation. It looked as though seers were taught to create a strategic situation in adaptation to their surroundings. It gives the impression that they waited for the right moment to spring a trap or to influence others, like jumping out of the bushes with machetes or something.

I decide, through observation, where to be or not be, and my perspective remains clear because I don't interfere with or distract my surroundings with my personal agenda. In this manner, I can still influence the outcome of my life, not because I manipulated it, but because I watched it and placed myself in the most strategic position.

Lujan:

That is one way of looking at this subject. Let me give you another. As you know, I am very proficient at kung fu. If someone were to attack me physically, my body would react without thought. It would respond to the circumstances and the pressures of that event, and it would do so in a way that was absolutely appropriate. It is at the point where your body realizes that you have been attacked that the true battle begins. During the assault you react without thought, but then you have to apply yourself to what happens after, and sustain that alert-but-empty body consciousness, without any preconceived ideas of results. That is where the real rubber hits the road, as they say.

You have to continue in your life as if it didn't happen, even though it has, thus allowing you to forget all accumulated residue and free your circumstances from preconception.

Be disengaged yet simultaneously fully aware, so that your body consciousness will intervene without the influence of the mind perpetually trying to calculate what is coming. Look at it this way: If there were a man around the corner waiting with a machete, I simply wouldn't go there. Your body knows, even if you can't conceive that you just avoided a situation; that's how it works. You know the battle that is at hand, yet you respond spontaneously and intuitively, in accordance with the pressure that is applied.

Bill:

Okay. I have more questions. Does everyone that lives an un-socialized life become a seer? Monks for example, Christian monks or Buddhist monks, or any monk, do they become seers because they don't live that programmed life? Or shamans, for that matter? What's the difference between being a shaman and a monk, in terms of seeing? Is it the physical systems you practice - such as Dragon's Tears - what makes you different from a monk?

Lujan:

That is an interesting question, for you know that I live similarly to a monk, and that I have the memories of a previous incarnation in Tibet. To answer your question: Yes, monks can be and often are seers, depending on what they do or don't do with what life presents them with, which will also define their fate. Your actions will determine your capacity to arrive at a point where you can say that you have really attained something, yet your achievements are not your achievements. This is a real contradiction. It is about what you do, but in the same breath, it is about what you don't do.

TEACHERS AND BENEFACTORS

Bill:

I have a question about teachers and benefactors. In other works about shamanism, there always seems to be the structure of teacher and benefactor. The teacher provides the verbal information, but there is a benefactor that seems to donate a portion of energy. You yourself had a teacher and benefactor. Is this structure necessary? You are teaching me and that seems to be working fine, but do I need to seek a benefactor?

Lujan:

I would say that the distinction between teacher and benefactor is that a teacher transmits something that can be grasped intellectually and a benefactor conveys something that can't be defined logically at all.

When you look at your experience with me, you are getting both logic and information that is unfathomable. The incomprehensible information must be assimilated into your being and become naturally organized in comparison to your innate power. You should have enough energy to incorporate the knowable and unknowable factors in the information I have given you. You have the capacity to connect to the silent reservoir in yourself and to be able to determine if your reasoning is getting in the way of that.

All my contact with the old Nagual and the others of his party did not take place in this world. If you read my first book you may recall that, I call all of them my benefactors, not just the old Nagual. But the teachers that have given me the most knowledge are the people I am confronted with on a daily basis.

If I determine my life with integrity, I still have to face the world in front of me. If someone acts without integrity, they still have to face the world that confronts them. The world at large is the greatest teacher and the people we interact with are part of this great lesson. In most cases, they show us who we are and whether we have personally applied ourselves correctly or incorrectly. In other cases they are just nutters. *(Lujan is laughing mischievously.)* You can never take control of someone or be certain that a relationship with him or her won't blow up in your face after some years either, because it may.

Everything we do has consequences and we can't really be sure of anything. This puts us in a position where we have to be humble enough to realize that we can only do the best that we can, but even that can come back to bite us in the end. Or it may not. This is our destiny as human beings. The truest teacher we have is the time we spend on this planet and how we utilize that time. There you have your teacher and your benefactor, your living circumstances and your own silent reservoirs of energy.

CRACKLING BEINGS

Lujan:

In 'The Art of Stalking Parallel Perception,' I describe a scene in which I was transported to a dream that was attempting to cater to my awareness by placing me in an old, antique car. The person that was there looked like my wife. She was pointing to the dashboard, saying that it was very beautiful. While she does appreciate physical beauty, for her to point out something like that, trying to draw my attention to it, is very unlike her, especially in dreaming.

I realized instantly that this was a projection of some other, alien awareness pretending to be her, and immediately voiced my conviction that it was not my wife. I was sure of this, and the feeling that arose in the dream was one of suspicion. So I expressed my misgivings and questioned the masquerade. This being was occupying my dreaming compartment and attempting to influence my perception by tauntingly indicating, through the façade of the imagery projected, that it had captured a portion of my wife's attention.

When we find ourselves in a dream, we must have the clarity to give voice to our intuitions, and when we do sense something, it will come as a bodily feeling of absolute certainty.

Upon inquiring I knew straight away what was occurring, as information is instantaneously transmitted between energetic beings and can be received in the same manner by a dreamer. If one has the sensitivity to intercept this communication, one can know exactly what the inorganic awareness is doing. The misgivings I felt towards this being alerted me to the deception, since I don't harbor any such feelings toward my wife.

The moment I voiced my realization, the dream scene vanished. Suddenly, another holographic universe was presented to me. The new world I found myself in was luminous. What I was seeing was the essential essence of the construct of the crackling beings. The entity that had drawn me there realized I had arrived at its nucleus with too much awareness and at once tried to distract me with the sound of an old phone ringing.

Upon hearing this manifestation, my auditory faculty, which is another point of seeing, began to use the sound to recreate what I knew from my everyday world. I knew this was a trick, since hearing is used for seeing. Our senses are manipulated in dreaming to visibly transport one into a familiar space, so as to fool awareness by creating a holographic image that appears to be physical, in response to the stimulus provided.

I went to reach for the phone, as one naturally would, and it was then that I realized I was luminous. The wave of energy that attempted to create the illusion of an arm reaching out became instantly obvious. I looked up towards the being, which was really crackling now, and the feeling I got in my chest was one of dread and disgust.

These electrically-charged beings are often the first to appear to a warrior when they follow the traditional path of dreaming, finding the hands and so forth. They transport the seer into their realm, which has been partitioned off from ours by an attention that acts as a membrane, cloaking their position within the universe, and there they cater to the visiting awareness in order to create a symbiotic bond. This resonance is not part of my energetic makeup, since I don't practice the old way of dreaming, so I was delivered straight to the heart of their world when I realized who they were.

Upon receiving that feeling of dread, my whole awareness swooped downwards and out of the cavernous structure we were in. Looking out into their world, I saw a cubic mass suspended in a vast, spacious universe.

The cube was dull and white, the color of bone. Gazing at it, I realized that a portion of my wife's attention was being held captive in that prison. At that instant I made the decision to retrieve her awareness and withdraw. Merely intending the maneuver was all that was necessary.

Suddenly I awoke in the living construct, fully aware of what had happened. I had ventured into an inorganic realm which I had no intention of exploring for I didn't want to be trapped or tracked in a world that would ultimately have no value in my life. The only thing of consequence in this dream sequence was that a portion of my wife's awareness was held captive there, which was a maneuver to coercively draw my attention into their domain.

The disadvantage that the crackling being had was that it didn't succeed to transfer my awareness into a living scene that would have represented the world I lived in. My only recourse upon finding myself in that realm was to be there as quickly and efficiently as I could, and discover why my perception had been transported to that alternate universe. I did just that and got the hell out. If I weren't lucid enough I wouldn't have been able to access the memory; it would have been even vaguer than a dream. As it was, I remembered immediately, but if I had been indulging in trying to dream, I wouldn't have had the capacity to retrieve that awareness. The experience simply wouldn't have been available to me.

Upon waking up I intended to move my wife's photonic potential back to her. She awoke with greater resolve and determination, now that this vital portion of her energy had been returned to her. Curiously, for weeks after this event my cheekbones and face were visibly changed in structure.

There were three scouts from that inorganic world that actively tried to subdue my personal power on another occasion. I began to tell you this story when I mentioned that I had a student who had three entities around him. These are the same type of beings and that scene I just described was where they initially became aware of me, and of my recognition of them.

After I visited their realm, they made an attempt to subdue my photonic potential by using what I would describe as an energetic cloak, similar to the veil they use to hide themselves, which they sought to place over my head. This cloak had a dual purpose: To repress my knowledge of them so that I could not teach others what I had seen and done, and to restrict my ability to see holographically within the waking world.

What these beings did was to try to transport me by grabbing and pulling at my arms and legs in dreaming, giving the sensation of bondage, in order to draw my energy down into the earth beneath my house. The way they went about this was to create a scene of extreme violence as I fell asleep, to cause me to fight against something brutal. This was to stop me from being as aware as I was in the previous setting and prevent me from being able to retrieve what I had taken, which was that portion of photonic potential which did not belong to them.

Understand that when I traveled to their world, I was within a visionary state of reception, which conveyed the truth of what was occurring. Alternatively, a dreamer can be catered to, and thus will not be able to discern what is really taking place due to their attention being fully occupied within the scenario set forth. This is the difference between a vision and a dream. Certainty within the second attention is a very difficult perception to acquire, but once established, is unmistakable.

The crackling beings also have the capacity to integrate with human awareness in the waking world. I described this in my first book, when I wrote about a Chinese man who sent a grey whirlwind to attack me in the living construct. They collude with individual consciousnesses by supplying seers with the illusion of power and thereby securing their dependence. Their basic tactic of catering to a person by giving them what they want, not what they truly need, is unfortunately a highly effective trap.

The result is that seers hooked by this bait are transported to worlds beyond their cognitive capacities, and when they die they cannot retrieve their photonic energy, which has been lost in these realms as a consequence of their insatiable desire for gratification. These entities feed on a seer's deepest wish for power and control. As you could imagine, this never ends well.

When I was watching these three entities trying to pin me under the house from the perspective of my photonic eye, it became clear that the fact that I was able to observe them meant that they had not succeeded in trapping me. In fact they were attempting to capture an image of me in a scene in which I was meant to become emotionally involved so that I would struggle against them, which would have meant the engagement of my photonic awareness. This is one way they can absorb our energy, which you are familiar with yourself, Bill. The danger of this is that if one becomes internally subdued in this way, the very memory would disappear but the residual feelings would remain. This strategy is similar to the technique that the dark sorcerer attempted with me years later in Bali.

As soon as I realized what was going on, I immediately disengaged from the scene. Once again, upon waking, the bone structure in my face was altered. My will power had also increased, not because I had taken anything from them but because, through that encounter, I was able to permanently disengage from dealing with these beings. From that point on, they no longer had direct access to me. That was the most valuable thing I got from this experience, for their interaction is by nature so complex and nefarious that it is extremely difficult to know what is really going on when one is in contact with them. They take the most clear and powerful parts of you and trap them in a place of fear.

By plucking even the minutest string within one's heart threads, they disrupt the warrior's one-hundred-percent fortitude through the disturbance that this interference creates. This unsettling frequency heralds the opening of a gateway that, over time, incrementally subdues the seer's attention if they do not become conscious of the coercive pressure being applied upon their attention.

The crackling beings are one of two principle types of scouts that humans encounter regularly in dreaming. Even though these electrically charged beings are not the main predator, which takes the form of the round shadow, keep in mind that they are nevertheless extremely dangerous. These types of emissaries exude an electric current, while one is dry and the other is damp. Through this charge they establish an emotional bondage of dependency and this is how the relationship starts, whether the dreamer remembers it or not. These inorganics, within the diversity of their universe, have cordoned themselves off, with an etheric stealth membrane, to hide from the main predator.

When I was living in Bali, I saw both of these beings from the cordoned-off universe, holographically projected in a silhouetted form, standing at the end of our bed, watching us sleeping. Although their electric configuration differs, they appeared in the same way: As very tall, shadow-like humanoids, similar to thin, black tree trunks. They hadn't actually physically entered our construct but their projection had. In Balinese culture these beings are highly integrated and are seen as gods. The veil between the worlds in Indonesia is very thin, so consequently their projections are seen as valuable artifacts that traditional sorcerers would have tried to tackle to absorb their power, which is extremely unwise. Once that connection is established, it becomes a lifetime engagement, one that will give them permanent access to one's inner world.

The dry being, when seen directly in energetic form, has a particular orange-yellow color that is very vibrant in comparison to the main predator, which is the true slave master of the human race. That predator often appears as one entity but is connected via a hive mind to a legion of demons. What one knows, they all know. The reason why I use this theological description is that this is the way they feel, utterly demonic.

There was one occasion when I directly experienced this hive mind. I had traveled to Los Angeles to speak with one of Juan Matus' old students, who was in his seventies at the time. Unfortunately I was a little too late, for he was very ill and dying by the time I got there. When I arrived, I met up with an associate who, unbeknownst to me at that time, had opened up an extremely dangerous portal. He did a few questionable things and when I confronted him, he told me that I had no idea what he had to go through because of this gateway he had accidently accessed.

Without going into the details of the circumstance, I said to him that there was no need to manipulate his environment and cause such discord. He informed me then that he must show me something before I proceed any further on my path, as a warning of what I will encounter if I persist. It was then that I realized he was a plant, a human pawn inserted into my circumstances.

He said that he would go to his hotel, five miles from where I was staying, and that he would ring me and send the awareness of the legions to me. I simply agreed and waited for his phone call. When he rang, he asked if I were ready and I said I was.

What I experienced at that moment was thousands of beings, passing through me with such speed that I was barely aware of the gap between each entity that entered my field of perception. The only thing I can say is that I was filled with the deepest sense of dread that I have ever endured. The overwhelming feeling was that resistance is futile, and that they have utmost control.

I recovered myself from the onslaught and told him bluntly to cut it out, that I wasn't impressed, and that upon leaving Los Angeles I would disengage contact immediately because of what he had demonstrated in sending this multitude towards me. In fact I was affected very deeply, shocked to the core, to be witness to this degree of symbiosis between the predator and a human being. I have not seen anything like it since, and never wish to experience such a thing again.

Bill:

That is one of the scariest things I've ever heard.

Lujan:

You're telling me. What's more, this shadow collective is not only in collusion with the main predator; they are absolutely interconnected. Also, the demonic entity with the scaly arms and red fingernails is equally linked into that hive mind, though its singular manifestation is ascribed to individuals' energy types. This allocation relates to a person's predetermined destiny in terms of their family line and the resultant preoccupations that govern their psychic profile.

Bill:

That's a lot to take in. I'm glad you told me about it but I have a feeling it's best not to dwell too much on the subject. I do have some questions though, about the inorganics I have witnessed.

Lujan:

Okay, go ahead.

Bill:

First, I think I have encountered the electrical dry type beings. Before I met you, I had read your first book and also works from other shamanic authors. One of the stories that got my attention had to do with pointing in dreams. The student in the story was instructed to point at objects in dreams if he wanted to see the object as it really was.

I awoke in dreaming one night and found myself wandering around in some foreign landscape, as usual. Suddenly, I realized I was not alone in that world. I found this odd, since most of the time my dream scenes are totally devoid of animated characters. When there are people or living creatures in the dream, it generally doesn't turn out well.

As soon as I realized I was not alone, I became very nervous. I looked up to see a big, fat goldfish slowly swimming or flying around the room. I had been trying out the pointing-at-things routine with no luck. Nothing I pointed at ever looked any different from before I pointed at it. I decided to try pointing at this fish. I did, and suddenly it burst into a bright ball of yellow light. It looked much like a small sun but it was accompanied by a furious sizzling sound. It sounded like an electric egg frying, if that makes any sense at all. The ball of light rushed at my fingertip and I felt heat all down my hand. I suddenly woke up and the scene ended. Was this the same type of creature?

Lujan:

It is the same. What was happening in those old sorcery stories was that the Nagual was telling his student to go into dreaming to search for artifacts in that world. It's important to be aware of the fact that these are objects left as a prop or point of entry into other universes, specifically placed to attract our attention. The problem is that those realms are not compatible with our sentient, organic awareness. What seers must realize is that this universe, the first attention that we abide within, is the only locatable dimensional matrix that our Double can enter so as to open up our universal eye.

The primary reason our Double has become so utterly removed from us is that our photonic energy has been utilized by a multitude of inorganic awarenesses, which piggyback as parasites upon our attention, so as to enter our organic reality via the vehicle of our human form. Through this antibiosis, our ultimate potential has been subdued within adaptive perceptual labyrinths. The form this possession takes will depend on which inorganic has gained access, and this affliction can be passed down the family line over many generations.

We humans are great anomalies in that we have awareness in both organic and inorganic forms. That is the magic we carry as human beings:

We are sentient from both perspectives. This puts us at a huge disadvantage in those dreaming worlds, however, for our organic awareness is very, very childlike. And our inorganic attention, our photonic projection, is equally as undeveloped, in comparison to the ancient universe that surrounds us. Like children, we are easily influenced by these alien energies, and through innumerable devices, they determine our reality for us when we are in their realm.

When this perceptual displacement occurs, we are automatically commanded to shift to a location with which our photonic energy is not familiar. Our photonic eye, which is the projection of our heart potential, then adapts and becomes familiar with that world. As we become acquainted with the dream scenes that are in front of us, if we are not fully awakened within our third eye capacity, the ability of these beings to manipulate our perception becomes staggering. They will show us what will most captivate our attention and what they present will be determined by who we are in this waking world.

Delving into these altered states gives us the illusion that we have the capacity to operate in such realms independently. However, this convincing perceptual maneuver is ultimately not beneficial as it is inextricably linked to the attention of the other beings 'helping' us to conceive of a construct that we would not be able to locate without them commanding us to open up to it. Once we get the impression that we have willed the dream scene to manifest, then these beings turn on us and incrementally shift our awareness to manipulate us to see what they want us to see, and that is not our command, it's theirs. This is why it is so dangerous to venture into their realm.

It depends on a person's power and nature as to which artifacts will become available to them in the dream realm. Specific artifacts are placed as props to catch certain attentions. Just like going to a museum, you will visit and view the artifacts that appeal to your character and taste. If you like Asian culture, you go to see that exhibition, or if you are more interested in Egyptian or European works, you will visit those sections.

Dream artifacts are no different. You will be attracted to them and they will be attracted to you, in regards to what you want and the reflection of who you think you are. Once you become involved with these artifacts, you will find the object itself has more power than you expected. It has the capacity to consume you in comparison to your innate energetic configuration. If you become occupied by that absorption, this will further distance you from your true purpose. This in turn is how you can be tagged and located by the inorganic that set forth the placement.

As with the pyramids or the Mayan hieroglyphs, or anything of that nature, the true significance of these ancient objects is not really clear to us now, and we won't know what their meaning is unless we really affix our attention upon them. The drawback with that is that once you become engaged on that level, you may discover something that is heavy and fundamentally incompatible with not only your individual configuration but also the current earthly alignment with neighboring celestial bodies. Such ancient gravity has the potential to disturb your energy field quite dramatically. It can take years to disconnect from a power object that has its roots in an attention that belongs to another era.

Bill:

Are the artifacts beings themselves?

Lujan:

No, they are holographic manifestations of intent. If you go into a museum, you see worldly artifacts; if you go into dreaming, you see dreaming artifacts. They are intentionally placed items in the dream construct. If you go there and point at something that draws your attention, it will come rushing at you.

Bill:

Like the goldfish?

Lujan:

Yes, like the goldfish. It was something that was placed there to do just what it did: Catch your attention. Then you became immersed in a reality that really had nothing to do with what you wanted or needed. It was just something you were interested in because of the information you were exposed to.

Bill:

So these things are there just to trap us?

Lujan:

They're there to attract us, and we become aware of them as our power reaches a greater degree of potency. When you get to a certain threshold, your teacher has a responsibility to advise you against proceeding any further. At this crucial juncture of developing your photonic awareness, you can find yourself in places that you may not be able to be retrieved from. If this occurs, the individual may return with powers of deduction that give the illusion of power. However, these warriors will find at the end of their lives that they will not be able to gather their photonic energy for their definitive journey, for it will have been consumed by the beings that installed the artifacts. Through such pursuits a seer's luminosity is exchanged for what seems like power, but which in the end leaves that warrior energetically bankrupt.

Remember, Bill, these artifacts are luminous projections with units of information stored in them. Everything within our matrix is a holographic manifestation and the dream realm is no different, but that alluring construct that seems like magic is really bait, binding you to the realm in which these beings await. These virtual objects are like doorbells to the inorganic world, leading you straight to them.

We readily find such artifacts in dreaming due to the possessive way we use our awareness to search for things in the first attention, or in our familiar world. Once we change the way we proceed in our waking life, then our inorganic world will automatically adapt and evolve in accordance. The artifacts have been there for millennia, but they too will transform in comparison to humanity and the individual warrior.

Bill:

It seems that most of the entities that exist are predatory and certainly don't have our best interest at heart. Would you say that the universe is entirely populated with predatory forces, as has been implied in other writings?

Lujan:

No, not at all. For instance, I have a black panther that for the moment journeys with me, which is an entirely benign presence. This being will act on my behalf without my conscious intervention and is completely autonomous. The panther is a product of the personal power of the old Nagual Lujan, my benefactor. This energetic manifestation was a result of his ability to be independent in the vastness that he traveled as a warrior. As he accrued strength, the panther, which became like a power animal to him, came into being and was eventually passed on to me.

That magical entity is a true reflection of who he was. In essence, he was so energetically adaptable that his photonic mass produced a counterpart that was inorganically based, yet intrinsically connected to him. You must realize that all of my benefactors were one hundred percent integrated with their Doubles, which is how they continued to traverse the unknown beyond their physical death.

When I was in contact with my benefactors, I was within the intention of a holographic realm that was not a dream scene but a direct product of their attention upon me. I was brought there and given instruction and, when that mentoring was complete, I was left with certain elements. One of the most distinctive features coming from this experience was the panther. This entity pounces, makes a sound, or appears around me when I am with my students. Even if I am on the phone with someone on the other side of the planet and there is an issue, the panther will intervene energetically to deal with the situation. She will send an energetic impulse that provokes the realization that there is no separation, even though I am half a world away. Her influence creates body shocks to jolt stubborn inertia and complacency.

This phenomenon, of an energetic manifestation coming into being as an independent entity that is wholly inorganic and powerful in its own right, has never really been fully elucidated in any shamanic writings thus far. Any intentions one has automatically contain within them the projection of the void itself, and the panther is what resulted from the personal power of the old Nagual. She came into being because of his desire to complete the transmission, to pass all of the necessary data to my being. Yet, even though she was the result of this intention, her actual manifestation reveals an entirely different phylum.

Such a degree of interdimensional interactivity presents quite a paradox to linear conception, if you consider the time span that occurred from when a portion of my luminosity was taken at seven and was simultaneously returned to me at forty. Although it was an ongoing transmission, my recall came to me in retrospective time capsules of memory that opened in correspondence with my readiness to access them. I can't really give you any other description than that.

Now the old Nagual is very far away from me and my Double is so close and these entities, including the panther, are starting to fade. They have become less useful. As my Double, or yours, or anyone's, gets closer, inorganic influence is always pushed away. Such connections are not viable or useful once we begin to merge with our Double.

We have no idea where this Double is or when we will interact with it, and when we do it is like a dream, but a dream of this reality. The true power of this reality is so far removed from what we believe is possible and that is why we get caught in so many inorganic realms, for we don't realize how much more we've got here. These inorganic beings offer us the promise of what we want to be, but that illusion is a poor substitute for real power. They take advantage of our youth in this universe.

Bill:

The black panther was created by your benefactor. Since I don't have a benefactor, then I guess I should not assume the entity that has always bothered me is something of power, or is beneficial to my awareness?

Lujan:

You know it is not beneficial.

Bill:

I agree, but it has always seemed to want my attention. This has always made a part of me wonder if there is a reason that it tries to communicate with me and engage with me. Is this something to take notice of or is it like a child trying to get me to pay attention because I ignore it?

Lujan:

This is very interesting. Behind the sound of your words, I hear the attempt to gain power or to take control. The way you ask these questions is leading me to answer you in a way that you want to hear. I could cater to you now and trap you in your own idea of your sense of power. I will not cater to you, Bill. These beings cater to you.

I will say, irrefutably, that the questions that you just asked me have to do with the need of this being to be fed, or to utilize your energy through your desire to be connected with it. You know its awareness has been detrimental already. You have told me how it distracts you and diverts your attention. Your interactions with this shadow are nothing like the interactions I have had with the panther. This entity has dealt with me very quickly and decisively, as I described in 'The Art of Stalking Parallel Perception'. By openly ambushing me, it presented the absolute demand to do what I have to do, or be stripped of the capacity to be connected to the energetic matrix; which was the power that was being presented to me by the old Nagual, in tandem with Juan Matus and the elusive shaman portrayed in the works of Carlos Castaneda who is known as The Tenant.

My very first encounter with the panther conclusively knocked out the residue of the social programming that had become embedded through a lifetime of interaction. It showed me that there is no way for me to proceed as a Nagual if I am not dead center.

You, on the other hand, are being hounded by something that is annoying and disturbing you, and you are trying to formulate an understanding within your own awareness, saying, "Is this equal to what Lujan has around him?" so that you can gather your own sense of personal power.

What you are attempting to do is to find out if this is an ally for you, and I would have to say no. I think that if you even ask yourself that question, you know that it is not. You know this because of the feelings you have gotten from this being, not to mention all of the answers I have given you already, which you have documented here. You have heard my story.

This situation is somewhat dangerous, for you are expecting to live vicariously through my experiences and to thus obtain what you desire, which is power and freedom. You actually desire the power of having the freedom to do what you want through being connected with this entity. I can assure you this is not power; this is a delusion that within your heart you know will not bring freedom.

You know, this is the danger of me elucidating my story, for it inadvertently beckons your need to attempt to emulate the power conveyed, through whatever makes itself available, before your burgeoning power is intact. In your particular case, the appearance of the shadow entity. Understand that previous Naguals may have unwittingly propagated misunderstanding by telling their stories, which have been seized upon and re-enacted by others.

We have already spoken about you and others attempting to re-live the old stories by setting out to tackle allies and take their power. I have also told you about how the panther was manifested by the integrity of the old Nagual. This ally was given to me and is quite independent of my own awareness. Like my benefactor, I have no desire to control this being or make it do my bidding in any way.

If I were obsessed with power, this creature would not be connected to me at all, since the old Nagual Lujan did not have an obsessive nature. If you obsess over the power that you think you are going to get from the being that is wreaking havoc in your household, this will cause your photonic energy to couple with it. Then it has caught you, not the other way around.

Here is where we have a departure in my story and in the path that most people go down. I was taken, kidnapped. I never wanted anything that I have been presented with. I wouldn't change the way my path has progressed as a Nagual and a warrior, but I didn't ask for any of it. Most people try to imitate the journeys outlined by others, and are so mistaken to want the unobtainable. In seeking to possess and replicate secondhand experiences one inadvertently misses their own journey.

At the same time, what you must realize is that by wandering aimlessly within these pseudo-pursuits, you are inviting yourself to be taken hostage by energetic sociopaths, in dreaming and alternate realities.

A lot of problems arise on the path of the warrior when people pursue the wrong things due to willful immaturity. Unfortunately the apprentice warrior often doesn't understand that what is ultimately right for them will take a lifetime to realize, and can only be accessed by proceeding with introspective observance and waiting for what necessitates their true path to appear.

This elusive emptiness is more difficult to intend upon than the pursuit of what one immediately desires, in comparison to what is presenting itself to you at the moment; for example, the shadow entity's influence. Self-realization is an extremely subtle and multifaceted process and this is the reason why it is so important not to appropriate someone else's story.

Now you see why I cannot responsibly provide you with what you want, for it would be a diversion from your heart path. I am in a very different position in comparison to the Nagual Juan Matus, in that I am extremely accessible to the public. His inaccessibility shielded him from the incessant demand of warriors to endorse their desperate need for validation as a substitute for wholeheartedly applying themselves and patiently waiting for real power to arrive.

This is my lot and I accept that, but you can't expect me to agree with you. Please don't take any of this personally, Bill. I want you to know that I am happy to be speaking to you about these things, but under no circumstances can I be put in a position where I allow myself to validate a warrior's delusions, for in essence, this will disconnect me from Spirit.

THE HEART OF HEARTS

Lujan:

Now Bill, I would like you to take a look at this well-known story as if it was an artifact in terms of your recollection of it. You see, what I am going to do now is give you a different version of what you have been told is a truth. The tale I am to tell will awaken a perspective that will speak to your heart and dissolve that solidified mindset which has been conjured into a belief system through repetition. Let's observe the story of the crucifixion of Christ and change your viewpoint so the artifact can become fluid instead of fixed.

When Jesus was on the cross being tortured, it is said that he cried out to the heavens, "My God, my God, why hast thou forsaken me?"

This seemingly simple account in itself is the first conjuring. The visual image of Jesus looking to the sky implies that he is addressing a powerful being, seemingly separate and apart from him, that has at this point withdrawn care and love. This epitomizes the predator's strategy, conjuring a fundamental dynamic of separation, abandonment and fear, and giving the message that we are divided, within and without.

In actuality, this man would have been looking down, into the hearts of those who loved him, they who were paralyzed by grief and dread, unable to voice their opposition to the atrocity that was being enacted, for if they did they would have been punished for speaking their truth by the governing forces who would have subjected them to a similar fate.

Simultaneously Jesus was viewing the corrupted hearts that believed their actions were justified. Here is where he realized how they had forsaken their truth, to the point where they were prepared to murder him, to extinguish something beautiful whose only purpose was to reveal where the darkness had stolen so much light.

Truly, what this man was saying was: "Oh my beloved, my heart of hearts, why dost thou forsake me?" What is essentially being revealed in this scripture is this question: "Why would the heart of another, which exists within all of us, wish to harm?"

You can see that this is an altogether different message to the one we have repeatedly been given. This deliberately corrupted portrayal of the divine is an overused stimulus to divide people and make us self-righteous, divorcing us from our innocence, which inherently recognizes unity. We must be determined to walk a clear path with heart, instead of being dragged into petty power struggles, which feed back into the illusion of duality and separation that further weakens us and blinds us to our true potential.

The foundation of dualism has been applied in so many different scenarios to control the masses. The central message being enforced over the ages is: Do what we tell you or bear the consequences. We are being herded like sheep via this ongoing cultivation of fear, away from our true potential: The realization of our heart of hearts.

When you are commanded to do what shouldn't be done, if you comply it is due to the fact that you fear the consequences of being harmed, ostracized or ridiculed. We have been so finely caged that we don't even know we have been caught. We see the cage, which is our corrupted behavior, as our freedom, as though it is our absolute right to operate from a covert and unintegral basis. A predatorial construct entraps us within our sense of self-righteousness.

Our rights really have nothing to do with the reason we are acting this way. Social conditioning has everything to do with the manipulation of truth to maintain control and hold our existence within a labyrinth so complex that the only way we will escape is to wake up to our hearts. We need to more deeply understand what is occurring within the matrix of our living perceptions, so as to free our selves from the never-ending loop of compliance being pressed upon us by beings, both organic and inorganic, that see us as an energetic resource.

With the three books I have written, I want to purposely incite resolution, so that people can come to an understanding of what's really occurring and realize that we have to take back our energetic sovereignty in all circumstances, whether in dreaming or in the waking world. It is time we came back to our central simplicity, our essential nature as human beings, which opens us up to a vast universal awareness that is our true attention.

Bill:

That was a beautiful story. It certainly got me thinking.

EVERYDAY ENTRAPMENTS

Bill:

You said you went to the realm of the crackling beings and retrieved a piece of your wife's awareness. There was another story similar to this where the sorcerer went to a dreaming position and retrieved a little girl. He got stuck there. Is this anything like your situation?

Lujan:

No. Unlike in the story you are referring to, I had not bargained with these creatures for years prior to my journey there. I was taken there, saw what was being done, took what I came for, and left very quickly. The consequences over the next six months were dramatic nevertheless. Their influence in my life was heavy, for they continued to interact with me through human hosts, which created extreme discomfort in a wide variety of circumstances. It was a concerted onslaught, as I witnessed their influence clearly appearing behind the eyes of those who would try to enthrall me within social dramas. That was a particularly intense period and in truth, this onslaught still continues more than twenty years later.

As a consequence, the information in my first book, about character assassination and living within your own power, was able to come through. Taking care of all of these types of things helps indicate to one when the integrity of the individuals that they are in contact with is or isn't intact.

You look at what is being done, what is being said, and where you are being led via the circumstance. This is how it works.

There are everyday traps that waylay our attention, and tap into our fertile reservoir of photonic or light energy. These inorganic booby traps in our collective construct are a very difficult subject to explain, which you are surely becoming aware of within your apprenticeship with me. Even when we become conscious of what is happening, we are still habitually surrounded. Unfortunately, until we are free, individually and collectively, we will be influenced by this insidious phenomenon.

We must first overcome ourselves and then overcome the complexity of ourself reflected within others. The trials and tribulations we are confronted with are never-ending. This is our lot to contend with, until the time when our bio-electromagnetic frequency shifts permanently into realities that wholly and solely relate to our connection with our Double and the multi-dimensional universe we are meant to be engaged within. When this happens we will become inaccessible to the inorganic predators that are enthralling our attention at the moment.

At this point in our evolution, there is a real possibility for many people to wake up to their true potential. As part of that process we must understand the real nature and complexities of the danger that we face. The necessity of transmitting this information is the reason I became an author and is why I am passing this information to you now, Bill.

We don't need to go back to old sorcery blueprints. All we have to do is to be centered within our heart's power, stand within our integrity and speak the truth of our circumstances, or stay silent when the truth can't be spoken. If we do this, then the light energy that is and has been taken from us can be returned and the influence we are contending with now will end. The intensity of our truth and the strength of our personal power will draw to us the strongest and only valid ally we have: Our Double.

The Double needs to be close enough to us to centrally locate itself fourth-dimensionally within our body. It will do this by racing at high speed from side-to-side through our physical form until our third eye completely opens. Then our dimensional matrix, which is our expanded human potential, will be revealed to us, first individually and then as a collective awakening.

The shadow beings do not want this development to occur, for not only will we grow to be independent of them but our inorganic potential will become so vast that their influence will never touch us again. That is why waking up to ourselves is such a monumental struggle.

Shadow beings desperately oppose our evolution and have installed corrupting mechanisms at every level of human interactivity. These undermining factors permeate our world, from the energetic undercurrents embedded within our social environment, through to the pollution and increasingly corporatized possession of all of our natural resources.

Virtually everything we consume has been contaminated with toxic materials that adversely affect our consciousness. The complex compounds, e.g., chemicals, which are increasingly present in almost everything that we purchase and sustain ourselves with, are defiling our bio-field, and have been introduced to 'dumb us down', by reducing our frequency so that we become more manageable. The fight for our freedom is at hand on every plane of existence.

Bill:

You said it! I am starting to realize the implications of what you have been saying about the old sorcery blueprints and the dangers of an immature desire to lay claim to power, especially in the context of the distorted perspective that most of us are operating from. What can you suggest for those who are seeking answers through the process of investigating what others have experienced, including yourself?

Lujan:

That's a good question. It is very important for people to understand that undertaking to appropriate a seer's information, via the vessel of a socially-programmed mind that wishes to embrace shamanism, can be quite a treacherous path, especially in the beginning. The introduction of expansive possibilities naturally leads us into unfamiliar areas, which is a good thing but also involves a certain amount of risk if we have been coercively maneuvered into a state of partial ignorance. The obstacles that we are faced with are quite complex, to say the least.

When an individual attempts to assimilate another's knowledge, they will very often seek to validate their position, in terms of their own progress and personal power, in comparison to what has been outlined. This will lead them to try to appropriate those stories, even though the full scope of the experience has not been imparted. Seers cannot deliver the totality of the wisdom they carry within any single transmission, since it is only energetically appropriate to transmit what is vital to the circumstance at hand.

Where a seer travels within their perception, they will never return again. When communicating the insights gleaned from those experiences, one can only speak to the occasion, which means different information will be forthcoming at different times. This is where it can become confusing to the initiate, since the obstacles that are confronting them in their daily life so strongly possess their awareness that they will only be able to access a minute portion of the wisdom delivered; hence the danger presented by the possibility of distortion and misappropriation.

The only valuable contribution we can offer is to directly share our vision and our photonic potential in the waking world, here in the first attention. The importance of appropriately communicating what is essential is exactly what Juan Matus conveyed within his original teachings. Juan Matus gave very clear lessons, but when his student obscured that wisdom through his own interpretation, this led to a tainted transmission being documented.

What I have been endeavoring to do is to communicate these central lessons without the influence of the second attention fixation. I have been giving you information without allusion to the archaic viewpoint that is a dead-end street. The only references I have made to the black sorcerers' way were to allow you to see that it is a trap. Many warriors today are using these old, half-understood methods to validate their positions as seers. They readily pursue this approach as a vehicle to their own power by catering to their own need to be recognized through that reflection.

Bill:

You mentioned shadow attention beginning with children and how it works to stop our seeing at a young age. Can you elaborate on that?

Lujan:

Like I said, all children are born with the natural ability to view the universe with their third eye. We arrive as natural seers, but this capacity is quickly obscured. Children often retain memories from infancy, or around the age of four to five years old, of seeing something like a little gargoyle type creature, maybe on their belly, or interacting with a sibling. The task of these entities is to establish the limiting agenda of the shadow beings very early on in our lives. Their purpose is to scare the young human to the point that they will no longer want to see with their third eye potential.

The acute fear of what the child sees causes an energetic shutdown. The only reason that these shadow beings can get to us as children is that the parents don't have the energetic capability to see or even be remotely aware of this intervening entity. When the parents deny the experience as fiction, what remains is the dread that memory creates, which drives the children away from external visualization.

Bill:

That makes a lot of sense, but you also mentioned the handing down of a social construct from parent to child. If the shadow stops our seeing as a young child then how does this social construct come into the picture?

Lujan:

The social programming finds an entry point when the shadow blocks the child from seeing the second attention in this first attention world. If the external visualization - seeing - is stopped by fear, then the young seer's visualization becomes internal. That is how the child's interior becomes infiltrated by imagery and incessant dialogue that does not belong to them.

This is the point at which the real programming of the parent begins, which not only inhibits the seer from within, but also establishes behavioral elements that do not benefit humanity at all. Here is where the social training gets applied, through repetitious example. This implementation is one of the prime objectives of the predatorial agenda, so as to maintain this limiting social construct for humanity as a whole.

Bill:

I can't help wondering, do you think that these entities you have been speaking about have a physical form in their point of origin in the universe, like we do?

Lujan:

No, they do not. They exist in inorganic form only. We are very rare in our duality, of inorganic and organic awareness. We base our perception and awareness on a physical perspective, but in fact most of the universe is not physical, as we understand it.

The universe originates from a place of dark matter, a place of nothing, or the void. These beings also originate from nothing or from the dark matter. They mimic our existence in order to cater to us. Theirs is not a physical realm you could go into. Even if you were trapped in their world for a lifetime or an eternity, the appearance of being physically bound is merely an illusion that is provided by their intention. These realms adapt in correspondence to our awareness and reflect back to us a holographic image that represents what we desire to see.

Bill:

Isn't this a holographic image we see in our waking world, too?

Lujan:

Yes, it is, but it is our human awareness that verifies our position within this matrix, which is for us to travel upon and evolve within. From the basis of the power that we obtain via our journey, we will discover our true expression in a multidimensional capacity. We are not completely integrated yet. At the moment we are still functioning in a very linear way. That is what the end of this Mayan cycle is all about: Embracing our full potential.

Bill:

What do you mean by, 'It is our human awareness that verifies our position within this matrix'?

Lujan:

We can recognize our human potential as the feeling that we are stationed within our heart and functioning independently, without any need to rely upon something else to substantiate the truths we see.

Bill:

So you don't think the world is coming to an end at the end of the Mayan calendar? Will we enter a new cycle of awareness?

Lujan:

Everyone will just go back to square one.

Bill:

Slowly, or all at once?

Lujan:

Well, I don't really know the answer to that. We will have to wait and see.

Bill:

All at once seems dramatic and would probably be devastating.

Lujan:

Everything within my life or from my perspective has always progressively grown and was never completely traumatic. This has been the case in your life too; everything develops. Even if you have an absolute epiphany, you still have to integrate the information, so you progressively move forward, one step at a time.

People need to remember that nothing will come and change the world for us. That is our responsibility, but everyone expects a savior of sorts. People are waiting for a Jesus or a Buddha figure to come along and change their reality for them. It is no one else's task to transform our awareness on our behalf. It's everyone's personal responsibility to take the information that they get from these types of leaders and apply it to themselves. Growth and evolution will always happen on an individual basis.

If enough of us live within our integrity, over one percent of the planet's population, it will have a shattering effect on the imprisoning principles of the general awareness of humanity. What happens will be a cathartic transformation, in terms of the current social paradigm shifting, away from what we are doing and toward what we should be doing.

HEARING IS FOR SEEING

Bill:

You made the comment 'hearing is for seeing', when you were telling me about the crackling beings. What did you mean by that?

Lujan:

Well, you see when you hear. Everybody knows that when you go into a dream you hear things, yet what you see in the dream will not likely correspond to what you hear. Your hearing becomes a visual anomaly. Hearing is a really important faculty, in conjunction with your feelings, to actually determine what you obtain within the dream as knowledge. This functionality within itself is a very complex factor that, if interfered with by a predatorial awareness, makes our journey all the more difficult if our power becomes displaced via that intervention.

In 'The Art of Stalking Parallel Perception', I discussed seeing my mother as she slept, one night when I was seven years old. When she awoke and saw me standing there in my sleepwalking attention, she rushed at me with murder in her eyes. This was the shadow. It had caught me witnessing its control over her while she slept, its manipulation of her dreaming attention.

What I was actually seeing was that shadow using the same language that she was accustomed to hearing to coercively create pictures in her dreams. These were holographic images crafted through its suggestive whispering. The frightening thing is that my mother is no different than most people on the planet who experience this every night when they sleep. To answer your question, this is how hearing can become seeing.

If you hear a sound that corresponds to a particular feeling, then the sound will recreate a visual image for you. It can even evoke smells that were in that environment for you at that time. The olfactory sense works in the same manner as hearing. All of our senses can recreate a visual scene for us or trigger second attention seeing. Every single ounce of our perception is for seeing.

When we are children, all of these senses are aligned and we are natural seers, but then we go into dreaming and the shadow whispers nightmares to us. We begin to switch off all of these innate capacities and we become the people we see walking down the street every day: Products of the shadow's installment of fear and the social programming passed to us by our parents who have been through this process as children themselves. Young humans mature and the cycle starts over again.

CLOAKED

Bill:

I told you the story of the three beings that caught me in dreaming and made me struggle against them. My story sounds very similar to what you described earlier. I have to wonder, did they trap me in some way? Did they succeed in pinning me in the earth somewhere or put an energetic cloak over my head? How would I know?

Lujan:

That's a good question, but the fact that you can ask it at all tells me that you have not been fully cloaked. If you had, you wouldn't even have the awareness to ask about it. Your ability to know is absolutely your responsibility, and if you had been cloaked or energetically buried, we would not even be able to have this conversation. This event happened before you found me, correct?

Bill:

That's right. That dream happened about ten years ago and I have been with you for about five years now.

Lujan:

Right. If you had been fully waylaid by these beings, your path would have never led to me. They wouldn't have allowed it.

INSTALLED FIXATIONS

Bill:

You said there are social traps that waylay our attention. What are some of these social traps?

Lujan:

They are installed fixations, like individualized prescriptions for behavior that inflame our illness, instead of allowing us to heal. The only relevant 'formula' that can be adopted to neutralize them is to apply oneself correctly to one's life. If you don't feel guilty, if you don't feel bad, if you have done the right thing, then there will be no regret. If there is nothing to lie about or to hide, then your perception will be clear. It's really quite simple.

Giving of yourself is also very healing. If you see that somebody needs assistance, you just openly avail yourself to the circumstance. This is being supportive of your environment. We all have to be naturally conscientious of what needs to be done, so that we build our personal power in terms of being generous, instead of being lethargic and irresponsible.

Bill:

Okay. So by living life like that, we start to gather our energy and personal power, and most people who go day to day with such unconscious behavior are not building their power, but instead are perpetuating the social program. So, in order to counter that, we need to bring our attention to our embedded negative conditioning, right?

Lujan:

Yes, but it is not that simple. Even when you start to behave in a way that is energetically responsible and good for yourself, you will still have to deal with other people, in terms of the coercive methods that are applied to subtly take you off your path by degrees.

Of course there are also those that will support and bolster you on your way. If you stay steadfast on your path with heart, you will become a clear conduit between the universe at large and others. You begin to reduce the karmic residue of those in your environment, by seeing them and by their truths flowing through you. You facilitate a form of release, and so grow more responsible as a human being.

This outlines the basic concept of karma. You reduce the other person's negative energy by virtue of the fact that you reduce the negative energy in yourself. Becoming a conduit means that you have to be free of your desire, for you realize there is something more important than you, but you also have to be centered enough to know that there are circumstances where you must take care not to put yourself in danger. This is a very delicate balancing act, to take this responsibility for the people around you and, at the same time, not become controlling or manipulative of those same people. It has to be natural, so you know where to be and where not to be, what to do and what not to do.

Bill:

I understand the definition of karma to mean that if you put good into the world, then good comes back to you, and if you do bad, then bad comes back to you. This is not a term I care for personally but you have used it here, so how do you define it?

Lujan:

What I am referring to doesn't exactly correspond to this strict definition. You can do things in this world with good intention and still cause destruction or bad effects. You can also do what you would perceive as bad and have beneficial effects come from it. I used this word because I needed something to help describe the situation of becoming a conduit.

When you become clear through cleaning up your life, you will be aware of everyone that comes into your environment. You will feel these people with your heart, so they become you. If they become you, then you have to speak their voice. The pressure they apply to you will cause your heart to become a mirror, reflecting their heart. You will start to speak their truth through the realizations that arise in you. They *are* you. They are your brothers and your sisters. We are one heart.

Once you become clear, you will start to give voice to the pressures that are applied to you through other people, and you will speak appropriately. By speaking and acting sincerely, within the power that you have and within the parameters of what you know can or cannot be done, you begin to release your environment of its fixations by just being aware of them.

You're a businessman, Bill. Let me put this into business terms for you. If one of your employees comes into work and they are not clear, your own clarity will alert you to this immediately. You know better than to take this person out into the field with you until they resolve these feelings, since they represent you and your company. If you go in front of someone else who is clear and sharp at business, they will ask themselves, "Am I going to go into business with these two individuals, when I can clearly see that his companion here has emotional problems that are unresolved and are brimming over into the circumstance at hand? Instead of being professional, it could become a personal issue with these two. Do I want to get involved in this deal with them?"

Bill:

You are absolutely right. I have had to deal with this many times, and if it is not handled correctly and immediately, it usually does become a personal issue that takes all the time and energy.

Lujan:

Business can't be personal, yet you have to be personally in business.

Bill:

That's a good statement!

MESCALITO

Lujan:

There are going to be a lot of people asking whether it is important to dream, or not to dream. The question is: How can we dream as true shamans?

The answer is that our dreams are relevant to a certain degree, as long as socially-ingrained imprints aren't transported into the scene itself. Once that import occurs, the dream is automatically corrupted with that agenda, which reflects back to us who we are and demands that everything that is encountered be transformed into the familiar elements of a socially-propelled consciousness. If these elements are not imported, you naturally become the unbiased witness and thus the dream becomes a vision.

A lot of people say, "I want to dream and it's my right to do so." There have been so many reports about the benefits of dreaming that a great number of people are determined to pursue this path. People who believe that, by going into alternative realms, they will discover the essential nature of their being are employing an erroneous strategy to pursue their growth as a warrior.

Going into an altered state of consciousness really only indicates that you have glimpsed the second attention. It is when you return to your everyday world that the real rubber hits the road. Your true power comes down to who you are and how you live. It doesn't have anything to do with witnessing other realms, unless you have the power to apply the lessons gained from those experiences.

A good example is your encounter with the man in the hat. At the time you didn't have the power to comprehend the full ramifications of that meeting. Nevertheless, this meeting was significant in that it pointed you out. As a result, we have discovered that it has created many subjects for us. Many of my students have been indicated to me by this entity. I will explain a little more about the man in the hat, and why it is infused in my living essence, in terms of traveling through other people to identify them to me. The man in the hat is Mescalito, the peyote entity, and I am a peyote shaman.

At one stage I owned around one hundred and fifty peyote. At this time it was legal to have these plants in my country of origin. The way that I engaged with this power plant was through gazing, and over a period of ten years I developed an extraordinary relationship with them. In many gazing sessions when I was looking deeply into the plants themselves, they would bob back and forward and sing to me. Eyes and a mouth would appear on each one of them and they would sing 'Oh Tee, Oh Tee', over and over and over again.

I was very attentive to their needs, in terms of water and sunlight, and it was quite an ordeal to carry each pot and put them in the sun for the period of time that they needed without them being burned. This was when the deeper relationship between these power plants and myself developed. They would send me a visual image of which one of them was too hot and needed to be brought back inside. What came with this image was a very soft whisper of my name.

I also had three that were grafted to San Pedro cacti and had grown to the size of grapefruit. These ones were very special. I used to take them and put them underneath my bed at night while I slept. Their energy field would engulf mine and when I was deeply silent and sleeping they would call me. The name they used to beckon me by was 'Mother'. We embarked on many journeys. It was a very magical time of my life, but as you know, all things come to an end.

On the last journey we took together they indicated that our voyages into the unknown were complete. At that point I gave them all away to good homes. This is the reason why the entity Mescalito is an indicator to point people out to me.

On one occasion, a friend of mine saw this entity as if it was walking down stairs, disappearing into the floor of his room. I don't pretend to know completely all of the explanations behind these appearances, and for this very reason all that comes from the contact indirectly is always saturated with magic. This entity has also appeared around Naomi Jean, watching her sleeping. When she told me about seeing this presence, I simply said, that's Mescalito.

HUMAN CONNECTIVITY AND NON-SEQUENTIAL TIME

Certain aspects of non-sequential time sequencing, in terms of our connectivity as sentient beings, are delivered to each of us in a staggered format that defies linear comprehension. You can observe how these anomalies may come about within the story of my mother, where she visited me at the point of her death. This was one of the two pivotal events in my life where she had a significant impact upon my destiny.

The other occasion was at the time when I was sleepwalking at the age of seven and I entered her room, and in my sleepwalking state I witnessed the shadow's attention whispering to her and guiding her dream scenes. When she lunged at me and woke me violently from my sleepwalking, she did so with such rage that it was shattering for me as a child.

As traumatic as this was, it was preordained. Her doing that became an artifact of power inserted in my perception that indicated the beginning of my path as a Nagual. It was here that my benefactor stepped in and stopped the advance of this shadow moving from my mother's awareness to mine. This was the exact same spherical entity that I described coming into contact with in my village a few months ago. At this later stage in my life, I had the power to witness it without losing my photonic energy to it.

As you know, our photonic energy is the light frequency that is the essential vibratory essence of a set of eyes that can perceive directly and is propelled primarily by the heart chakra. The heart center can see, just as our feelings, our hearing and our other senses can see. Everything about us has an eye to it and, when these are combined, this becomes our photonic potential in dreaming. It is our perceptual faculty that traverses the universe in non-organic form. I hope this is not too complex or hard for you to comprehend because this is the most direct way I can explain the way it manifests. Some things are not reasonably comprehensible and seeing must be known for what it is upon its arrival.

When my mother died, her life force came to where I physically was. She was riddled with cancer at the time of her death, and this I saw in the vision, for I had no contact with her later in our lives. When going into a visionary state such as this, one knows with concrete certainty that what is seen is exactly what is meant to be absorbed through that encounter. One can only appropriate what is delivered within the immediacy of that moment.

When I saw her lying there, I realized my second stepfather was lying next to her. He had died about ten years earlier. I never observed his energy leaving the planet at the time of his death. I found this strange, as most of my family members have visited me as sort of a port of call as they leave the earth, to allow me to say goodbye to the most pertinent part of their being.

I actually saw my first stepfather's death about fifteen years before he died, which is extremely unusual. I have written about this in 'The Art of Stalking Parallel Perception' when I discussed following a man through the process of him leaving all of his holdings, and painfully witnessing all of his attachments and regrets. It was quite a horrific experience, in fact, and it took me some years to realize whose departure I was viewing, since he was not actually dead at the time.

My second stepfather was an agent in World War II. He was a very interesting man who had encountered a great deal of responsibility along his life path. He did quite a lot of things to help in the conclusion of that war, but those experiences had left him riddled with guilt. The events that had impacted his life were pinned all over his being and were leaking out of his energy field. He was in his late fifties at the time he came into our lives and I was just a teenager. He was a very alert and highly-strung individual.

He ultimately died of leukemia, which is a very uncomfortable way to go. My mother had not really attended to him in a way that was appropriate as he neared the end of his life. He needed her to be there, one hundred percent, in a way that would procure the comfort a person craves at that crucial point in between life and death. Their journey together was mutually heartbreaking, in that they did not manage to totally embrace one another, for everyone at the end of their life needs to focus on where they know they are loved. He didn't have that love, that nurturing that he so desperately needed. Their experience of physical death was devastating for them, for they were faced in that moment with all the extraneous artifacts that had accumulated throughout a lifetime.

She too was very frightened and disillusioned in the end. She went through a very similar lonely desperation, and at the moment of her departure they conjoined in the realm where he had been waiting in limbo for her arrival. Here is where they simultaneously communicated the vital composites of information that relayed to each other that they had finally understood the full implications of how they had conducted themselves on their life path. It was only in their final moments that this realization came to light, after having wasted so much precious time within senseless pursuits.

During their meeting, I observed their communication and my being simultaneously expanded into the field of their mutual communication, exuding my gratitude and appreciation for what they had made available to my being as a young man. This forever released me from the binding force that is the karmic effect that would have inevitably brought us together again. This same phenomenon has occurred with all of my family line that have passed over, thus setting me free.

There is a reason why I am reiterating this story to you. In previous sorcery teachings, it is stated that one must leave their family to find freedom in order to cultivate inaccessibility to familiar elements that bind the warrior to their personal history. What I have just described is one of the methods by which this instruction is meant to be implemented: Not through the seer's willful act but through the natural influx of eternity that beckons resolve and provides the opportunity to sever karmic ties appropriately, upon the moment that arrives.

Apart from visionary experiences such as that which I have just outlined, a warrior may also access these pivotal moments within the living structure of their waking world. There comes a time where one's circumstances reach a crucial point of culmination, and the warrior will realize that certain relationships have expired, before death even occurs. The complexity of that scene will determine itself in comparison to the mutual pressures one arrives upon.

One should never be advised by another to leave their family, for in essence, this will deplete one's personal decision-making capacities, thus stifling that imprisoned individual's connection to Spirit through taking on an erroneous instruction. The force of eternity will present the chance to bring completion to karmic cycles, and upon this point, the seer must choose to proceed in accordance with that dictum or suffer the consequences.

The journey of my parents shows how tragically wasteful life can be when one does not consider the full implications of their responsibility on this journey. When the two of them died, they were alone and in pain, faced with the dilemma of being confronted with all that was unresolved within their lives. This last port of call showed them that even though they reached a point of energetic resolve, they would still have to implement this understanding within their next lifetime, and deal with all the complexities that come with that. It is vital that a seer's life is lived with integrity, for this will determine the power of their next incarnation, should they return to physical form.

I know this doesn't make sequential sense, since everyone died at different points in time, and me living with them as a young man doesn't really correlate to the vision. Yet these events are all interconnected and bound by the multidimensional aspects of our human condition. What you must realize is that this story reveals how we are all intimately linked within the seen and unseen aspects of our universal attention. Once we come to terms with the fact that our awareness has been waylaid by a shadow agenda that propels us to act with Machiavellian selfishness, we can move away from this self-destructive program. We are designed to function with an acute amount of consciousness that reflects our true connectivity and in time, we will.

REINCARNATION OF THE OLD NAGUAL LUJAN

Bill:

The other day you made a remark to me that after reading what you have written here, you feel that some of the concepts may leave the reader confused and don't seem to come to a conclusion.

Lujan:

I did. I feel that these subjects may be confusing at points for some people. What I'd liked to say to those who may find the material inconclusive from a socially-determined standpoint is this: The narrative will lead up to a point at which people will ask, "Where am I?" and then they will be left with themselves. This is the way we usually function in life. The end is never really a conclusion. The only thing that you can travel on is change. If you find yourself at a point in which you ask yourself the question, "What's next?" in most cases, there is no answer. You have to wait for the substance of your life to culminate to a point of understanding about what really was, in terms of what is occurring at the moment you witness it.

Bill:

Still foggy here.

Lujan:

(Laughing at me.) There is a method to my madness, Bill, and a reason why I am explaining this. When I was a young boy, around the age of seven, I was deeply affected by the presence of my benefactor, unbeknownst to me at that point. Once, I was in the bathroom and I watched the water spiraling down the sink. At the same time, my Double was standing on its tiptoes, on my bed-head. I was frightened to the core. Behind me was a black void and I knew that if I fell backwards, it would consume me. I sensed that I would never return. In front of me I saw a swirl of colorful, fibrous lights that looked like they wanted to paint themselves into each other and which pulled me in their direction. I was precariously balanced in between the two, in a very strange state of awareness.

It was only when my father came and saw me standing there in a trance, and poked me in the shoulder with his large calloused finger and said, "Do you know who you are?" that I came back to my physical body and realized I had been simultaneously watching the tap water run down the sink. I calmly looked up into my father's eyes and said, "Of course I know who I am," and walked out of the room, leaving my family bewildered and perplexed. They thought I was crazy, but they had no idea what was really going on.

This was the first direct contact I had with my Double, and I was seeing through its eyes. Here is where you must understand that our capacity to see from a photonic perspective, in terms of actualizing visions in our waking world and within dreams, has wholly and solely to do with the power of the Double. When we have experiences of déjà vu or the complex visualizations that we see within dreams, this is our photonic projection from our heart center, reaching out to beckon our attention to recognize our full potential. This is truly the basis of our unbending intent to be self-actualized, which is focused toward our central matrix, via the power of the living presence of our Double.

This is the very reason that I have given explicit warning about the danger of these eyes being stolen by predatorial awareness and re-appropriated into the dimensional matrices of inorganics, via dream constructs and the active illusion that presents itself to us within our waking world. The secret of our Double, which was revealed in the story I just outlined, is that when it is close enough, its presence begins to dimensionalize our living construct, thus interfering with the sedentary matrix and delivering the seer to the source of their own magic.

Bill:

That all seems a bit heavy for a seven-year-old.

Lujan:

No doubt, but that was the influence of the awareness of the old Nagual Lujan. It was around this time that he intervened at my first stepfather's house, with my mother. There are many, many stories that need to be shared and corroborated from where I have emerged. A lot of the information I have may seem quite contradictory until it is completely understood through one's own experience, but that is just the way it is.

I relayed to you that I lived as a Tibetan man and that when I died, one of my students tended to my body, in preparation for the burial ceremony, so that my awareness could travel from its current position to its next point of being. In the Tibetan tradition, they employ chanting techniques, which evoke certain frequencies that have the ability to sustain the awareness of an individual in transition. This does not hold them in a stasis, but prevents them from being interfered with during this shift, so that they can recalibrate the most pertinent elements of their memory in the new continuum they arrive upon. When I journeyed to that lifetime, I actually absorbed his memories, which were rightfully mine, through that dimensional visitation.

When I was obtained by the old Nagual Lujan at the age of seven, I was taken, or kidnapped, if you will. My awareness was transported by the vibrating frequency of his attention into that elusive continuum known as bardo, which a person's awareness passes through on the way to its next port of call.

When my benefactor came into contact with the shamanic lineage of the Central Americas, he was introduced, by the Tenant, to the highly refined perception of how to sustain oneself within that attention. He thus gained the ability to make dimensional jumps in order to sustain the treasures that he had obtained throughout his lifetime as an oriental shaman. When he passed over, he was able to maintain the most crucial elements of his awareness and remain lucidly in contact with those memories, until his reemergence.

Bill:

Reemergence from what?

Lujan:

From this state into the next body he would be reincarnated into. This relates to what I explained about when my wife and I realized that we came through the void. We knew that this moment was a recommencement. We could see the beginning and the end. It was a culmination, a point of arrival. What I am introducing to you and everyone else is that we are non-sequential beings. We are non-linear. We are highly dimensional. You can't grasp and understand these things from a reasonable perspective until you know and realize that this these temporal transmutations are occurring in your own life.

The Dragon Gate movement system that I teach is specifically for reconnecting us to our multidimensionality. It has been stripped of ritualistic aspects and reduced to the bare-bone practices that shift awareness. When students perform these movements and are confronted with the silence that they create, they are facing that subtle state of being. If a shaman becomes accomplished enough, then at the moment of their death they pass through bardo and will be able to decide to keep the awareness they gathered from their life, or not. I chose to transfer these movements and teachings to this lifetime for they are a treasure. These forms are of immense value in terms of bringing silent gravity to our awareness.

We are dimensionalized and we are here to move fluidly within the multifaceted matrix of our human potential. A clear heart and empty mind will allow things to be seen clearly, in comparison to one's power and the energetic momentum of one's life path.

Bill:

So bardo is where we are all headed?

Lujan:

All human awareness passes through this point in our universe at the time of death. Most people have not stored enough energy within the actions of their life to hold themselves in that state. They are flung out as quickly as they enter, and their memories are relinquished, for they have been consumed by the voracious beak of inorganic awareness.

Bill:

So it is possible to store enough energy to stay there?

Lujan:

Yes, but one would need to have an enormous amount of personal power and gravity to hold their traction.

Bill:

You mentioned, in 'The Art of Stalking Parallel Perception', that there is a group of people there, your benefactor's cohorts. You also say that they helped teach you. Besides aiding in your instruction, was it their collective power that allowed the old Nagual Lujan to maintain traction in this state of awareness long enough to exact his maneuver?

Lujan:

Exactly.

Bill:

So obviously, that realm can be entered before death, because you're still alive.

Lujan:

A portion of my awareness was taken there at the age of seven. Usually what happens is that a young person is taken away from their family by a group of seers that possess the information that will educate a new Nagual. This traditional way of training a Nagual was not available for me for two reasons. First is that the old Nagual did not exist in physical form in the year that I was to be taken. Second, even if he was there physically, can you imagine my family's reaction to an old, white-haired Asian shaman showing up at my door and telling my parents he was here to take their son away to be given a portion of his awareness and power, and to become the next Nagual in his line?

Bill:

That would have been a funny scene!

Lujan:

An alternate maneuver had to be employed by the old Nagual. Traditionally, a group of his acolytes would have come to my parent's door and requested that I come with them for the transmission of the old Nagual's awareness to me. This would have never happened in our modern, Western world, so this is why a portion of my energy was taken at the age of seven, and kept for thirty-three years. This facet of my photonic potential was transported into this subtle state that I have described to you, and instructed there by my benefactor.

The feat that the old Nagual accomplished is extraordinary. He took an individual's awareness from the first attention into that altered state, and sustained it there for what seemed to be thirty-three years in my life, but was only a few moments to them. In all actuality, the portion of my energy that was taken was returned instantly, though it took me those thirty-three years to assimilate the information and to come to terms with who I was and what my path and purpose here was. I lived and grew into this information from a child in the realm that my benefactor had introduced me into, while concurrently absorbing that very same wisdom in the waking-world.

When he split those time capsules and put me in those different positions, he was teaching me, but really I was educating myself. These maneuvers were mentioned in 'The Art of Stalking Parallel Perception', and now are being fully explained here to give people the rock-solid vantage point from which they can look back and start to understand such possibilities. Nevertheless, it will be hard for people to fully comprehend in the beginning, since this way of reaching through time has never been revealed in this light.

I will always see the old Nagual as my benefactor for that is the truth; he was before me, and now, I am humbly before him. Without gratitude and humility, how could I possibly be myself?

I am living in a Western man's body now and if people have had experiences with the old Nagual Lujan, they have had experiences with me.

He was able to traverse space and time to land here in me to begin a new lineage of awakened seers. I am the old Nagual Lujan.

Bill:

So a shaman can gather his awareness, cast it forward, and make a leap through time to bring his awareness and information to a new era?

Lujan:

Yes. And there were extensive discussions in the 1960s about another man that could do this, known as the Tenant. What I am outlining now is to give further information on how he achieved these feats. The Tenant prefers to remain in this very subtle state of bardo, so he very rarely appears in human form.

These seers had the capacity to travel extensively on the universal vehicle of the third eye matrix. Past, present, and future were available to them, not only of their lifetimes but of the lifetimes of others they were to inevitably be in contact with, e.g., me. The Tenant traveled upon the awareness of each Nagual that came after him. All the lessons he imparted were direct transmissions that were lived within, which became one's life experience as if it was a memory. As each Nagual grows the information within that experience expands, as do all events that we engage within.

This is exactly what you do, Bill. You live your life, you absorb the experiences, and they become you. The only difference is that the intensity of the gifts of the Tenant are equivalent to a lifetime's engagement, though they were transferred within hours or days, or even moments, of contact. It is for this reason that many of the Naguals were apprehensive about the gifts that they would obtain from him, for they knew that the transmission would readjust their perception irreversibly.

Seen from this perspective, when the Tenant obtained boosts of energy from those he educated to sustain himself within bardo, his gift was equal to the amount of photonic reserve one would have to outlay in their lifetime to obtain such wisdom. So there was never a loss through this exchange; there was ultimately only a gain.

In actuality, the Tenant was giving very generously and speeding up the evolutionary process of each successive Nagual through this energetic transmission. The only downfall that comes about from this type of teaching is that if the apprentice still possesses artifacts within their attention that could be detrimental, these may expand and consume the seer within a fight for their very life in terms of which aberration becomes magnified with the power of that transfer.

These transdimensional abilities are some of the very powerful gifts that the Tenant imparted to the old Nagual Lujan, my benefactor. The two of them were inexplicably linked through mutual affection. This is how the strange anomaly occurred of the interlinking aspects of our existences, which have amalgamated into a multiplex that unifies.

These are the only explanations that I could possibly impart to explain how the lineage of Juan Matus has been affected via the wisdom obtained. The Tenant and the old Nagual Lujan conspired with Juan Matus to travel upon the future incarnation of myself as an abstract continuum, which I have experienced and now am transmitting to you, in terms of conveying the understanding of the diversity that a warrior may and can obtain in their lifetime.

Bill:

You've mentioned artifacts again. How can artifacts change the course of people's lives?

Lujan:

Artifacts are points of reference within a person's perception that have to do with the original propulsion of their attention. In actuality, they are fixations that are part of their socially-conditioned response, which become embedded and gain diversity as the person matures. To put it plainly, these artifacts flourish within the vehicle of emotional states like jealousy, possessiveness, anger, self-pity, pride, and other such tendencies. These states become possessively guarded artifacts when the person uses them to focus their intention to get what they want.

How this works is that the emotion itself, through obsessive practice, sustains the person's perception within it, and that intention then becomes a sorceric tool that they use to navigate their reality, thus propelling their attention as a usable item within their field of influence. Such maneuvers adversely affect our reality, right down to the atomic flux.

Internally stabilized emotional reference points can be utilized tandemly to keep the connective links between these elements alive, thus solidifying collective self-importance. These are first attention artifacts. Of course there are second attention artifacts that are provided by inorganic influence, which obviously use the first attention sites of the warrior, but I have explained this extensively already.

What the Tenant has done, as far as contact with me, is to allow people to become aware through these descriptions that we are making dimensional jumps, and that we are forgetting where we came from. We are not meant to relinquish our awareness so completely. At this point in time we are supposed to be opening up to the vast possibilities of human perception, through accessing the wisdom of our many lives' experiences. This is why it is so important to identify the predatorial agenda and disengage from it, so we can live up to our true photonic potential which, if strong enough, will allow us to remember everything and to know what we have to do, for our power will be in place.

At the moment, we don't know where to go and we don't know where we came from, and that is the problem. We are being led, instead of being self-empowered, self-directed individuals that see what needs to happen in our environment.

LOOKING FOR THE HANDS IN DREAMING

Bill:

I have a question about some of the more common teachings on shamanism and dreaming. Why does the Nagual teach his apprentice to look for his hands in dreaming?

Lujan:

The reason why this was taught was for the initiate to become acquainted with their second attention, or photonic awareness, in a lucid dreaming state. Once this first stage is arrived upon, the warrior is carefully observed to see which internal elements come to the forefront in regards to the accumulation of their lifetime preoccupations. If they have drawn to themselves extraneous artifacts that divert them away from the central heart of the teachings of the Nagual, then this will have to be addressed before proceeding any further. If not, these dominant fixations will color the perceptual horizon and thereby steal the eyes of the initiate, blinding them to the essential truth that is before them.

It is not enough to travel upon the initial achievement alone, as an ability to enter into lucid dreaming does not indicate disengagement from the predatorial agenda. A warrior's journey is more than just a dream that solicits the idea that one has power before even escaping the influence of what is barely comprehended. Seers must check themselves continually.

Unfortunately many warriors are taking a chaotic approach to realizing their potential by trying to explore and master dream constructs that are all-consuming and, paradoxically, equally as dimensionalized as we are meant to be. Hence their seductive appeal. To access our genuine potential, the dreamer has to let go of the fantasy, the illusion of achievement in hypnotically absorbing worlds that twist human attention into a shadow of what it could be.

Those very dream constructs, in which the dreamer feels they have found freedom, supply them with a sense of false bravado. They then bring this arrogance back as their experience and report their journeys as if they were scouts into the unknown. In reality they are only purporting the parameters of the holographic prison cell that they moved within. The spurious sense of power that a warrior gains from these dreaming experiences distorts clarity to such a degree that, as a result, the reasonable premises of their intellect take over. They bathe in the illusion of their own sense of grandeur and forgo their inner silence.

Upon returning to the waking world, these dreamers are saturated with the covert insertions of the predatorial agenda, which are embraced as if that were their own identity. Thus they become trapped within a loop of consciousness where they have to be right at all costs, even to the detriment of others. The reason for this is that the predator feeds into the consciousness of the dreamer and distorts their sense of self to such a degree that they can no longer see the natural ebbs and flows within the world around them. They are blinded to the subtle communications of the holographic universe by the disproportionate sense of identity that has replaced their emptiness.

For the average person who simply arrives in dreaming without the particular desire to use this attention to gain something, this distortion is also applied, yet is not as obvious. It is those seeking power who are catered to extensively so as to ensure they will not realize that their idea of freedom is actually their capture within those chimerical realms. This is very difficult to recognize, for nobody can see their own trap, which they have actually built in symbiosis with the parasite awareness.

When this method of perceptual traversing is introduced and the warrior starts to become familiar with the all-encompassing potential of their true attention, the next phase to be carefully negotiated is the need to develop the clarity necessary to focus their photonic eye within the second attention without succumbing to the corrupting force of the habitually-embedded conditioning that has accompanied them up to that point.

Without this lucidity, the Double won't have the capacity to focus its power upon the central matrix of the initiate, so as to awaken the true introspective sight that will create the gravity needed to draw it into close proximity.

Dreaming is essentially a practice ground for the apprentice to introduce their second attention into their first attention consciousness, so they may begin to apply the externalization of their photonic energy within the living construct.

When the dimensional faculty of seeing appears in our living reality, the initiate is confronted with the first perceptual territory with which they may not be familiar. Manifesting visibly as the transportation of holographic imagery into the waking world, this becomes the practical application of the third attention, which in turn alerts one to their fourth attention endowment. This awakening will be supplied through the conjoining of one's current cognitive abilities with the interdimensional aspects of the Double's power.

The significant difference between activating our dimensional capacities in the everyday world and in dreaming is that here in the living construct you cannot practice creating or influencing the imagery. You must wait for the holographic visions of the third eye matrix to appear. Simply put, introducing a seer to these far-reaching possibilities is the reason why an apprentice is instructed to look for their hands._

In doing this, you are not seeing your real hands, or the hands of your Double. What you perceive is a representation of the memory of your human form, seen as a holographic image by your photonic eye. What you access is manifested by your own heart's luminous potential, in tandem with the unbending intent of one's physical eyes. This in turn is inwardly inverted and through this process, imagery is transferred, in coiling figure-eight motions, to the internal visual cortex, thus activating a multitude of spinning matrices that represent the inner doorways to our universal attention.

Although many people have focused extensively on dreaming as a means to accumulate power, there is really no need to fixate one's awareness within escapist pursuits. Once this aspect of our photonic potential is accessed, we are not meant to linger too long in this area of the second attention. We are meant to bring that awareness into the waking world. It's a very quick, concise lesson.

So you come out of that experience and you practice your dreaming awake here. Then you start to solidify your third attention capacity and to realize your potential as a human being by manifesting those possibilities in waking life, as your true human dimensionalization. It is a process that will take a lifetime to fully realize.

LUJAN'S DOUBLE

Bill:

You mentioned once to me that you had contact with your Double. What actually happened?

Lujan:

When my Double revealed itself, all kinds of metaphysical manifestations occurred, and they were in the waking world, not in a dream. This was after decades of applying the practices I inherited.

It was right next to me and I was having information downloaded into my central matrix, my fourth-dimensional access point. I could see great distances and view sentient beings, animals and insects, in holographic forms. They were larger than life, emanating the essence of their being-ness as clearly as if they were right in front of me, though they were actually many miles away. I could see through the walls, and was observing the people in the unit across the way, who were making a lot of noise that night and had awoken me.

I decided to sit up on the end of my bed, and that is when I saw it, a mirror image of myself, right beside me. The influence of my Double had saturated the room, and time and space had merged in a way that I'd never experienced before. I was being given instruction in physical movements, and simultaneously listening to my Double speak about worlds within worlds. It was pure communication on where it had ventured. The room was filled with a beautiful golden hue and everything that I explain now had already happened, even though I was witnessing it occurring.

The Double's voice was imbued with so much power. When I listened to its utterances, the sound of hundreds of thousands of voices was focused on one point. The origin was boundless, infinite, endless, yet contained. Every syllable reverberated with an awesome gravity. My body was filled with so much potential, so much power. I've had my Double close to me before, but never like this. Communication was simultaneously coming from multiple universes, and I assimilated so much from just one sentence. This is our natural state of being, which we have lost touch with and must now remember.

Hearing the Double's voice, I was filled with joy and silence and the feeling of so much power. In that state I knew I could do anything without regret, and loving elation was absolutely abundant. How to apply this state as a permanent way of being was one of the major lessons imparted to me during this encounter.

It was here because I had amassed enough power for it to approach. I knew that its presence was in accordance with a need for it to take guardianship of my being. It was time that I no longer be injured by predatorial awareness, and in order to protect me the Double gave me a sequence of movements that I have called the 'Guardian Set', which I inserted into Whispering Palms. These movements will beckon my Double to come to my aid in the later stages of my life.

After a timeless moment, it vanished, and the room returned to normality. So now I await my next encounter. All I can say is that communication with our Double far greatly exceeds what one can achieve in the second attention. Upon its integration all of our memories, our lifetimes, come flooding in, along with a tremendous amount of speed and lucidity. By virtue of this encounter I have gained access to my memories of so many different things.

HUMAN POTENTIAL VS. PREDATORIAL PROJECTIONS

Lujan:

There is something I would like you to be aware of.

Bill:

Sounds interesting.

Lujan:

I gave a full description of my time in the Dream Maker's Realm in my first book. Of all the teachers that I interacted with there, the Nagual Juan Matus, the old Nagual Lujan, and the Tenant were the only real entities. They taught me many lessons in that state of awareness, and one of them was the ability to recognize the human energetic signature.

The most direct way I could learn to identify genuine, human, photonic potential was to encounter the avatars that my benefactors projected from their Doubles. Any time I met anyone other than those three, I was interacting with holographic manifestations of their intent. This very particular training gives one the ability to distinguish between a true human signature and the signature of projections originating from a predatorial source.

You have to understand that the wisdom transferred from all of these avatars was very pertinent information, even though they were holographic by nature. When I was with Lucien, Somai, Barak or the four women, the interaction was training me to recognize human photonic energy manifested as scouts. These projections were employed, exclusively for me, to train my second and third attention potential as a Nagual.

Another of the many gifts that I obtained by being in their presence was the ability to open up my third eye matrix to hundreds of positions in order to communicate. I became absolutely aware how to fan out to multiple locations as a holographic projection. How this usually manifests is that an image of me will appear in circumstances as if I am looking through a window. This phenomenon has been experienced by many of my students. Some, like Leia, have seen a projection of me materialize in their room, where only my upper torso is visible and I am gazing at them. When this happens I absorb information I need to access, whether I remember the event or not.

When people come to see me and are in my physical presence, I access information directly from their photonic energy field that allows me to see what their real human potential is, and where they are trapped in terms of the predator's agenda.

Perceptual traversing of this nature also gives the seer the ability to contact other third eye matrices in the universe, other energetic beings more akin to us, so that one can access pertinent information that goes beyond our current paradigm. These sentient beings are not interested in coming and taking us away in dreaming or hijacking our second attention. They care about our progress, though for the most part we don't acknowledge them or realize their historical influence upon our evolution. Nevertheless, evidence of their input is mapped out all across the leylines of our planet, the significance of which has been carefully veiled by the powers that be.

Such entities exist within our living construct as energetic projections from another part of the universe. They are here and are attempting to contact us, and could be denoted as alien. We must fully awaken to our potential before we can appreciate the scope of this very subtle plane of communication. Once we become aligned with this frequency then we will be capable of making direct contact with these beings. This won't occur while we are energetically inept.

I was trained in this specific way so I could relay the information necessary to give warriors the capacity to pause long enough to witness the insidious symbiosis that has poisoned our human consciousness, turning us against ourselves, and thus each other. When the purpose of those projections from my benefactors was fulfilled, the energy of the holographic potential of Somai, Lucien, Barak, Dyani, Mion, Shashani and Ela was then absorbed into my third eye matrix.

This is how the gift from the Tenant was transferred, through the memories obtained, while I was de-compartmentalized in the realm of bardo with my benefactors.

Bill:

So they were not real people?

Lujan:

They were real in the sense that they carried luminous encoding that pertained to our true human nature. These projections contained information within the light frequency observed. The fact that they were created by my benefactors made them absolutely distinct from an emanation generated by an inorganic awareness. The complexities of this influx were not obvious when I was first introduced to them. It was only years later, when the byproduct of that photonic absorption began to develop in me, that I realized what had happened.

The Tenant conveyed this information in order to transmit the ability to recognize human potential above and beyond the predatorial bias, which is projected through the host. In essence this means that when a seer is navigating through the vast sea of awareness that we are confronted with on a daily basis, they will be able to distinguish, through reaction and interaction, our true photonic frequency, in comparison to the subterfuge we have been subject to.

The only way that I can explain this in practical terms is that when interacting in the first attention, the seer will see the negative agenda afoot, which belongs to the predator, yet ignore it and remain fully devoted to the human part.

When interacting, observe very carefully until the time that your energetic input is necessary. However, your observational involvement can only be applied a few times; otherwise you may provoke an unwanted influx that will make you unnecessarily accessible, thus vulnerable. If a person does not have enough discipline and energy to self-regulate via this contact, then it becomes necessary to quickly withdraw so as to not become involved with the never-ending loop of social drama that is set forth by an imprisoned individual.

Unfortunately, in most cases the warrior has no option but to disengage completely from communication with people whose conditioning is stronger than their determination to evolve. Even ten to fifteen years later you may discover that they are still looping upon the same imprinted behavior, through repetitive affirmations that confirm to themselves and their allies that their social madness is justifiable.

Withdrawal is the only compassionate thing that can be applied in these situations. The warrior simply innocently watches the person trying to set them up, knowing it is not the true human potential that is acting. It is the predator, stalking one's circumstances and attempting to undermine the warrior's purpose and fortitude so that their photonic energy will be consumed in unnecessary drama.

Sometimes this gravitational eddy becomes apparent in the form of a holographic scene, and at other times, one sees it behind the person's eyes. You will sense that the individual in question knows what they are doing; that is, lying on behalf of the predator within them. One can acknowledge the human element even while simultaneously being targeted by covert predatorial projections. The seer may also perceive a network of corruption being cultivated under the auspice of transferal to another person, through the soliciting of repetitive consensus that goes completely against our sovereign nature.

On many occasions the warrior may have to ignore the agenda, even though it is recognized, and at the same time love the human aspect, hoping it will come to the forefront. However, as the warrior matures on their path, they will realize that, in most cases, their efforts to sustain themselves within untenable circumstances are absolutely futile, and that at a certain point, they will have to withdraw entirely, for nobody in their right mind can put up with such insanity for prolonged periods. You will inevitably learn through experience.

Once you gain vital distance from internalization of the predatorial influence, you will see every variance and nuance of what comes toward you. As you get older and more experienced, this sensitivity becomes more refined. It takes a lifetime to fully understand the extent of what the predatorial mind is doing with our human potential. My eyes have slowly opened as I have developed. Our awakening is not something that happens all at once. You don't just snap your fingers and find that you are complete.

My benefactors' maneuvers were so refined and specific that it has taken years of observation for me to come to understand. The projections they generated were holographically real enough to engage my attention and, as a result of this contact, if ever I am caught in the second attention I will know what is a true human scout and what is inorganically inappropriate, no matter which universe I am in.

These are difficult lessons to understand intellectually, for they were enacted in the second attention. I share these stories with you to show you how a seer can be trained in that state of awareness. Upon becoming conscious of these factors, the only true responsibility we have as sovereign beings is to identify what part of us is truly human and what part is predatorial, so that we can advance beyond the entrapments that are destroying our planet and inevitably our species along with it.

If a predatorial attitude prevails, humanity's ultimate potential will be annihilated. Through that holocaust, the great surge of photonic energy that is meant to be used to journey beyond our present location will be absorbed by a corrupt attention, which in essence represents the continued enslavement of our species.

Bill:

How can we reduce this negative influence in our lives?

Lujan:

Firstly, eat organic fruit! And lots of it! *(Lujan is laughing out loud.)* Seriously though, you need to detoxify your system so that your physical body can reach a high enough frequency to observe what I am about to explain.

If you want to combat corruption in general, the first thing you must do is hunt this all-pervasive presence within. It is essential to become aware of the part of you that is influenced by the predator's mind; which is the element that reacts. We must discern what is necessary and unnecessary in our lives so as to determine our true photonic potential, which belongs to our heart's path. Pursuing anything other than that is folly.

Each individual will be delivered by their circumstances into the lesson they need to learn. Be aware that at any point you can bring light to your situation and move on, without regret, or add darkness, and forever be haunted and pursued by that perception.

When it is not our heart that we are operating from, we can be sure it is the mind of the predator working within us. The most superb strategy that can be applied in a military situation is to persuade the individual that they are acting upon their own will, when really they are being directed by the enemy. This is what the predator is doing with humanity. It has taken our minds and our hearts and imprisoned them within the idea that it is our rightful sovereignty to conduct ourselves in the insane manner that we are currently accustomed to. We all need to cultivate inner silence to escape this collective fixation, which is essentially maintained through one's internal dialogue.

Know what is human and what to talk to, and what is shadow and what to question. Speak to the true human heart and attempt to extricate yourself from the agenda at hand. It is up to each individual to discover where this influence is within us, and then to recognize where it exists externally in the world around you. A seer must learn to identify their true authenticity in the context of the circumstances they find themselves in.

Bill:

I understand what you are saying about predatorial awareness; it is becoming self-evident. What I would really like to ask is: How am I being trained in comparison to the way you were taught by your benefactors, in bardo?

Lujan:

I subject you to the same frequencies that I was subject to. What happens with all of my students, and especially my apprentices, is that I identify your true human potential and you realize it. A Nagual locates where the predator's agenda is flourishing and where your social anchors are connected to that. Then you learn to look within yourself, to recalibrate your attention in comparison to the circumstances that confront you at every moment you arrive upon. We cooperatively push the predator out, one social construct at a time. Beyond that instruction, your evolution is ultimately your responsibility.

RECLAMATION

Bill:

I've been thinking a lot about our ability to 'photonically project', as when remote viewing. I can't help wondering if it isn't happening all the time, without our realizing it. Is it? And, if it is, why don't we remember?

Lujan:

As you already know, remote viewing is a facet of our capacity to be in a non-ordinary state of consciousness, or shift dimensionally, in terms of recognizing the characteristics of what is coming, or what has been, in the moment in which we have arrived. That is part of our third eye capacity: To use déjà vu as an indicator towards the development of a potential path that is manifesting. A lot of people do experience this consciously but tend to immediately brush off the event by saying "Oh! Déjà vu!" and then completely forgetting about it as they only have a very vague idea of what that actually signifies.

What the warrior has to become aware of is that we are in contact with our future through this particular facility, even though we are still waiting for it to arrive. We patiently attend what will appear in comparison to the multitude of variations that may make themselves randomly available to the seer. Unfortunately the functionality of the predator's mind confuses this innate faculty. This is the real issue that I am endeavoring to help you understand.

The predatorial awareness can enter our world and peer through the eyes of a human being, in essence to destabilize circumstances, if deemed absolutely necessary. In other words, if an individual is finding their center, the shadow injects itself through a human host and reestablishes its corrupting influence by creating drama through emotional imbalance. This input has exponential effects, spreading throughout the environment and multiplying through activating familiar resonance.

Everybody has had the experience of looking into somebody's eyes and seeing a snake lurking in the background, ready to strike. This venomous perception is the predator, peering through the vehicle of the host's consciousness, in which it has assiduously cultivated those characteristics that allow it entry. This presence is especially noticeable in those who have nasty vindictiveness embedded within, who secretly covet others' circumstances, effectively stalling another's progress through the games set afoot by these so-called 'personality traits' that have possessed them.

The predatorial view relocates a person's inner awareness within characteristics of shiftiness so that its presence cannot be identified. It seems to be the person himself that is concealed, but in fact it is the predator that is so well hidden. Such placements are masked within a range of behaviors that are given credibility, for we have been taught to think of them as natural, socially-acceptable attributes. This commonplace corruption in essence is an illness that many human beings carry within them like a virus. We've been programmed to ignore this presence and anyone who speaks about it is deemed totally paranoid. If you do, people will say you've lost your mind, and in a sense it will be true; for you will have lost the predator's mind.

Remember Bill, if you experiences any disruptions to your heart centeredness, either internally or from an outside influence, you can be absolutely assured that possession is afoot. Unfortunately, in this day and age, such affliction is propagated through the idea that it is normal to be permeated by covert behaviors. Yet this social consent has taken us so far away from our true human nature.

We've been slowly, coercively moved into areas of acceptance that are truly inacceptable, through an accumulative contamination of human culture. It is a global contagion that spreads insidiously on a contained frequency that holds the human biofield in stasis, effectively disallowing our true potential to flourish.

You want to know how to develop your photonic potential and what you can do with it. This is an indicator that you have gained a certain amount of freedom and are slowly reclaiming your true mind.

It's really very simple: Take all your circumstances and turn them into the warrior's way. When you encounter others you look within yourself, for you are them and they become you. This is the union that we have forgotten. We have been separated from our eternal nature by our belief in duality.

Under the guise of individuality we struggle to assemble the puzzle, for we identify so strongly with this point of separation that we have forgotten to listen and see and look for the reflection of ourselves in all circumstances. We can and must make obsolete this false premise by recognizing that we are unified, and thus never bringing harm to one another, for this inevitably brings harm to ourselves.

I have been developing your photonic potential, Bill, by speaking truthfully from my heart and relaying that truth directly to your heart, so your personal power is growing as a result of genuine human communication. As this is happening, my stories are becoming your stories, in terms of your internal imagery expanding to encompass the possibility of your true potential coming to light. They become your visions and your reality. They become your truth.

As your truth grows, you ask me questions that are reflections of this growth. Through our natural communication we transfer luminous information, which enhances both of our photonic potential. This is what is meant to happen on a grand scale. This is how humans are made to communicate, at all times. Even though it may not seem like you are developing anything, you really are.

Through learning how to interact mindfully, and disengaging from divisive behaviors, you align with your true self. All that has been partitioned off from your awareness begins to return to you. Although the complex manifestations of socialization will present endless challenges to one's determination to evolve, there is one simple way to navigate this labyrinth:

Speak with your true voice, from your heart, and you will bring release to your circumstances so that the manifestation of truth can appear.

POSSESSION

Bill:

You said that the 'pesky shadow' is trying to integrate with my energy. Is it anything like the demon you described? What other experiences have you had with this kind of thing?

Lujan:

I want you to recall what I told you about the time when I encountered the round shadow. I was sleeping, and my photonic eye opened to the world around me as I sensed the pressure of the predator in my environment. My photonic eye became my ability to see within the reality I am living in. This composite of the second attention viewpoint within the first attention is our third attention perceptual capacity.

One of the ways that dreaming awake occurs is that, while slumbering, you are one hundred percent functioning as a conscious being, yet your physical body can only see the ceiling and the room around you, while your photonic eye can travel in the waking world.

When I went to see what the black inorganic was doing, I was using this potential, which is the amassment of my photonic energy in my heart center. The heart center is automatically connected to what is called 'shen', or your spirit. Shen is etherically situated in the region of our forehead.

There is a form of viscous light energy that is always located there when we are strong, clear, and complete. This energy augments our third eye facility and gives us the simple capacity to 'see' what is in front of us.

You remember I told you that this black sorceric being was collecting the essential whisperings of everyone in that area. As I drew closer to it, my luminous field became aware of its true location. It was not a scout of any kind; it was here in this reality.

Upon my approach, I was relayed the imagery of all the negative social behavior that this creature was absorbing from the sleeping people in the area. It was harvesting the electromagnetic intensity issued from all of their prevalent doings, which was leaking from their energy fields. By collecting their life force, it amassed strength. It was not too dissimilar to a witch lurching forward as a shadow upon a wall, with long, boney fingers to snatch one's innocence. I experienced this very phenomenon in Bali.

I was teaching a woman a gazing technique and, as we were proceeding through the clockwise rotations to discover the essence of blue luminosity emanating from a plant, I saw, from the corner of my right eye, a sinister shadow leaning forward to touch me. I quickly turned and said to my student, "You have a witch upon you."

As I spoke, the shadow quickly recoiled deep into her energy field, to hide within her etheric layering. She asked me, "Aren't you scared?"

I said, "No." Yet simultaneously my whole body became covered in goosebumps.

Bodily responses of this kind are one of the ways that you can discover a hidden entity within someone's luminosity. Your body tries to escape and a strange revulsion, mixed with fear, alerts you to a sinister presence. Predatorial manifestations appear in many forms, and hide in obscure places. That particular witch was eventually extricated, through very similar techniques to those that I prescribed to my other student who had the Southeast Asian entity piggybacking on his life force.

That night, as I approached the magnetic emanations of the round shadow, I realized that if I went just an inch closer, it would suck my energy into it as well, and I would lose the memory of seeing this being at all. Since it could not embed itself in my energy field, as it had done with others, it had no recourse but to attempt to steal my photonic eye.

It wanted to capture this capacity from me so that I could not relay to you, or to anyone else, what I had seen, in all of its myriad manifestations. I more than realized the turmoil that this creature was cultivating within the people around me. If I allowed myself to lose my composure within these confrontations, I would be swept into the drama that was being played out.

I watched and kept my distance, as I knew exactly what was happening. The predator was integrating in the consciousness of the villagers to create a narrow corridor of surreptitious exchange where it could slyly slip past my guard, and attempt to induce an emotional response on my part, through ensuring the insertion of petty problems in daily life that would cause undue stress. This being was herding their awareness, intending to paint me into a corner, so to speak, because of the information I was releasing. This insidious process is how our photonic energy is drained by the shadow being's degrading input within the internal landscape.

What keeps these placements so well hidden is that this very installment in turn becomes the illusion of a person's intelligence; in other words, their ability to maneuver, manipulate, and reposition themselves in order to create conditions favorable to the realization of covert agendas, which are the predator's signature. This is shadow stalking. It is essentially a stealthy, relentless assassination of the fortitude and evolutionary characteristics of humanity.

All this takes place through the furtive insertion of the predatorial mind, implanted within the consciousness of the people, who can't fathom that it is not they themselves who initiate this social drama, even though they are fully conscious of what they are doing within their enactments.

By sharing my stories that outline the links to the associated behavioral patterns that indicate possession, I am alerting you to what may possibly confront you in your future, so as to eliminate the possibility of your photonic eye being stolen through the many different applications that the legions may apply.

UNFATHOMABLE EQUATIONS

Bill, throughout our contact I have always warned about the coercive elements that sway our attention. Within the context of writing this book, we have returned to this subject over and over again. There is a very good reason for this.

Before I go into that, I would like to further elaborate on the story of the woman that came to me for shamanic healing, the one that had a witch hidden within her energy field. I want to make it very clear to the reader that positive resolutions abound within our existence when the sincere application of our personal integrity is given the opportunity to establish its true boundary, which alerts each individual to the appropriate and inappropriate applications of oneself within their personal environment.

When my student was lying on the treatment table, face-up, I ran my thumbs across her forehead, to her temples. As I performed this she opened her eyes and gazed at me. From where I was standing, she was upside-down. As she looked at me, her brown eyes turned silver. Viewing this from my perspective was shocking. Her smile looked like a grimace.

"Why aren't you scared?" the witch from within her exclaimed in a wretched tone. When I did not respond, she closed her eyes, and when she re-opened them they were brown again.

After the treatment, she revealed that she had been to Tibet and asked a lama to release her, and that when he saw these eyes, he ran out of the room screaming and said that no one should touch her. She traveled to many countries to find a solution, but to no avail. She also said she had lost many friends due to this entity's influence.

When she had finished explaining her dilemma, I said to her, "It is my lot to see and bring resolve to these circumstances, and to transmit the understanding that will release you, and everybody else that comes in contact with this knowledge, from these nefarious entrapments."

The way that I proceeded in order to detach that particular entity was by applying a star gazing technique, which we did together for three nights in succession; thus liberating her from that possession.

In the case of the man that had the Southeast Asian entity connected to him, we were unable to perform the same technique during his visit, due to cloudy skies and the fact that he had to leave the day after to return to his country of origin. Unfortunately, the pervasive influence of that demon had saturated his attention to such a degree that he needed me to assist him in dislodging the entity from his biofield, for he did not have enough energy to do it alone.

Once away from my presence, he was so heavily manipulated by this being that he lost grasp of our connection. It became impossible for his inner seer to discern the folly he was playing out as acts of black magic, which in actuality was the application of the power of the entity within his personal circumstances.

Even though this man was possessed, he still had the capacity to make a choice to free himself from the binding applications of the entity's input into his reality. It was his reluctance to give up on the supposed power that came from his manipulations that ultimately bound him to the demon. Once the extent of that possessive attachment became apparent my only recourse was to withdraw completely, hoping that he would eventually wake up, and that the people around him would begin to see through his coercive behavior.

By elucidating these circumstances directly to you, Bill, I am outlining one of my tasks in this life, which is to reveal the dilemma that we are faced with as human beings and offer insight as to what is actually occurring. The portion of your apprenticeship which has been put down in writing will inform and empower those who read this material to realize that they are in a position to make simple choices about how to proceed in life.

Everything that has occurred, every step that is taken, from everybody's perspective, is never a mistake, but a decision that each of us makes upon the moment that we arrive. It is crucial that you, and everybody that becomes involved within absorbing this very fundamental premise, stand very still and listen carefully.

I have spoken extensively about past lives, the intervention of entities, and the moment that we all arrive upon, each of which inevitably affects our future within the multifaceted aspects of our continuums. This most vital equation of our fractalized nature is not obvious until we realize it.

Now I will relate to you a story, an event in my life that was as powerful as meeting with my Double. It represents the consequence, the multidimensional ramifications, of the Double's consciousness, which is interwoven, interdimensionally, with all of our lifetimes, whether they be future or past events, or coexisting timelines. The Double is the key to us waking up to all of these staggered equations.

Only one central factor is of importance: Our connection to Spirit. If a warrior is one centimeter off 'north', the power contained within that delicate connection is lost. To maintain that precious connectivity a shaman is absolutely compelled to act in accordance to the dictums of Spirit, that subtle communication that indicates how to proceed. A lack of comprehension of the implications of this binding imperative is what makes it difficult for some initiates to understand or accept the finality of the acts of a man of power.

I would now like to introduce everybody to the second crucial symbiotic point of Spirit that a warrior discovers upon their journey, which I have not spoken of until now.

I recently had a life-changing experience. This event solidified my previous knowing in terms of following the dictums of eternity no matter the consequences upon my person.

It seemed that the path was harsh and arduous at certain junctures of my life. I was continually faced with the choice-less choice, for to act with absolute integrity was truly my only recourse, come what may. Many sorcerers have opted to endorse agendas that, in the end, severed their precious heart link with Spirit and subsequently assured that as long as their influence was prevalent, the individuals they were in contact with would never become aware of this elusive factor.

This is why it is so very important to stand firmly and witness all events unfolding as they should, and never influence this process with any form of agenda, nor concede to another's need to be validated so as to cushion oneself from the inevitable onslaught that would ensue from standing one's ground.

As you know, anything other than a seer's truth being applied ultimately pays into shadow attention. There are grave consequences to our actions at this point in time, and I hope this will become plainly apparent throughout the story I am about to relay. It is a time of awakening. We now have the opportunity to align ourselves with something greater than what has been available to us throughout the duration of the 26,000-year galactic cycle coming to a close, yet signifying a new beginning, at the end of 2012. The experience I am to share with you now revealed to me the exact ramifications of our personal alignment within our human continuum.

I woke up within a vision. It was the first time in my life that this had happened so clearly. It was the year 2512, and I was in a subterranean location. There were four of us working together and upon witnessing that scene every ounce of information regarding the nature of our living purpose became available to me. We were organizing four magnetized, rectangular objects that looked like dark granite, and whose edges were extremely inconsistent. I can best describe them as rippling, like water.

Though they were all of equal mass, two of them were elongated in comparison to the others, so that when they were placed together within their configuration they once again resembled a rectangle. Depending on which surface was organized to face the pertinent direction, their magnetic force would create the vortex necessary to calibrate alternate alignments within the time-space continuum. The aim was to travel back to my location, five hundred years before.

The feeling that I received when viewing myself and my purpose in the future gave me a sense of elation that united with my current understanding, from a bodily perspective, and this infusion enhanced my personal connection with Spirit, by absolutely confirming that my life path is being traversed in alignment with my true destiny.

On this occasion only three of us were to journey. The fourth traveler was to stay behind. It was imperative that, upon the point that the vortex opened, his physical form be behind the barrier that was positioned to protect him from the peripheral momentum. The reason for this was that if his body were subject to the whipping edges of that centrifugal force, outside of the direct proximity of the continuum becoming available, his physical form would be extinguished.

Unfortunately, for reasons only known to his pre-determined destiny, he didn't make it in time back to the area where his body would be safe. So consequently, he simply vanished and turned into a luminous sphere of light. As we disappeared on our journey to the location that had been organized, I glanced back and witnessed him leaving his point of origin, which, paradoxically, did not exist.

From my future perspective none of us has a point of origin, yet our locations are defined by our purpose. By writing this book with you, Bill, the doorway to my future has opened, simultaneously bringing my past to an instant that is a culmination of both my present and future purposes combined.

I would like you to listen very carefully to what I am to say next.

Imagine you have one focal point in existence that determines your future and your past. Currently I am in this position.

My actions determine my future, which in turn defines the outcome of my present moment, my present lifetime.

Now I want you to imagine that you have the power to align your future and your past events from where you stand, and that, as your Double approaches, you have only one point of calibration, whose implications are multi-dimensional in terms of who you are here, now.

If you diligently follow the dictums of Spirit, your future will arrive as a dimensional continuum, for your Double will be drawn into close proximity by virtue of your personal integrity being applied.

Firstly, your past lives will rush in. This is significant, but a warrior can be swayed from their path even once this influx has occurred. If this diversion takes place, the consequence will be that their most potent potential future will not become available in terms of their own internal galactic alignment.

This is why I have doggedly hit your consciousness, over and over again, with the implications of shadow attention, simultaneously reminding everybody who reads this book that with every decision and action taken there is a recalibration occurring.

Upon these critical access points, one can draw to themself the most powerful equation, which is their future, aligned with the most appropriate past, so as to awaken to what I have just described and finally move beyond this crucial threshold. The key lies in our application to life itself.

So in essence one can bring many futures and many pasts to this moment, this pivotal event. Finally the true aspect of free will is being handed to us all and our destinies will be determined by our choices.

THE UNIVERSAL EQUALIZER

Bill:

Most of what you have explained makes sense, but I have to admit, I still don't fully comprehend a lot of what you have taught me. Much of the reincarnation and multidimensional information is like studying algebra. I understand the material, but I don't exactly have any direct use for it, as far as I can tell at the moment, nor do I have much personal experience with which to create a reference point for the information. Simply put, it is neat info, but I am not sure what the practical application is and, quite frankly, some of it is scaring me on a really deep level.

Lujan:

It is very interesting how you describe your understanding of this. I am in the exact same situation, in that I too must evolve from where I stand, regardless of who I am and what I know. No matter how far we've come, our circumstances always equalize each warrior's position through the challenges that avail themselves to us at the moment we arrive.

What you perceive as my advantage is that I've connected the dots within the sequences of my lifetimes, where you yourself are on the verge of connecting these variances, and this may seem intimidating to you until you are fully awakened. But let me tell you, you and I are so much the same.

We are all faced with the dilemma of which way to proceed. It is simply fundamental: The rule of rules. Everybody must go through his or her own stuff.

This morning when I was doing my practices, I could see through my arms. They were jelly-like in their appearance and had a metallic feeling, as if I were made out of mercury. The floor beneath me was spinning, as if at any moment I would fall through it. I looked up to my dear friend, Lee, and explained what was happening.

"That's fantastic!" he said with a huge smile.

You know, Bill, though this kind of thing may seem impressive, it is insignificant compared to what is really important, and that is to listen, and love, and understand your circumstances, and travel upon the true matrix of our human communication: To live it without illusion. When this is fully embraced, then I'll happily fall through the floor and disappear.

What I'm wishing to convey is that you have before you the opportunity to be sincerely authentic, within the parameters of your present perceptual location. You must embrace what you perceive as your limitation, for within this challenge lies the key to your freedom. There are no exceptions to the rule. It is the same for everybody.

You are attempting to acquire the calculative maneuverability to comprehend what I have brought to your attention, so that you yourself one day can impart the very same nuances. Don't be concerned, this will come about of its own accord, gradually and not as you would expect.

For instance, you might say that you remember what happened to you twenty years ago, and it has taught you to do this or not to do that, but can you connect the dots for someone who is twenty, when you are forty? Perhaps you could stop them from making this or that mistake on their path, but most of the time you just have to let people go through their own trials and tribulations, so that they can realize their own potential. You and I are in this situation right now.

Let me give you an example. You know very well what it is you have to do if you want to be successful in business. You can give one of your employees advice on how to proceed, and then watch him go off and do something totally different and maybe apply himself erroneously. He will venture out on his own steam, following his own tangent, which is borne of his passions in regards to his own life path. You can't save him or educate him. You just have to let him go and learn those lessons.

Will he ever wake up to the information that you relayed? You won't know until he arrives upon the truth of those realizations himself, and in any case your life paths may diverge before that occurs. Upon witnessing this feedback, should that opportunity arise, you will understand that every person is meant to encounter what their fate has in store for them. Everybody has to come to terms with the contradictions that outline their own personal continuity. This is why one must let go and allow eternity to unfold in due course.

Now, you say that you don't comprehend, but I know you are wrong. You are performing in a supernatural manner at this very moment, as is everybody. You just need to realize it. If you were not seeing in this manner already, the universe would not be creating the pressure on my heart center that allows me to present this information to you. We wouldn't be having these discussions at all.

You also say that this is like a mathematical equation that you understand but can't apply to your life, but that's where you are wrong. You have to realize that we no longer live in rainforests; for the most part we are urbanites and we have to work with what we've got.

When someone comes to do business with you and they are carrying unresolved emotions, you receive an indication, don't you? You see a scene or an image that reveals their intention, or you catch a signal from their eyes or their body language, right?

Bill:

Yes, usually.

Lujan:

This is an example of the holographic universe communicating with you, and of the manifestation of your third eye applying itself. You see the circumstance for what it is and you just know things, and you are alerted to the agenda at foot. The important thing is to remember what you've seen, and to know what you are waiting for, though it won't be wholly apparent until it manifests in its entirety.

This is our universal equalizer, and we are all in the same position. You are not only understanding what I have told you about your multidimensional aspects, but including them in your actions on a regular basis. You can see what's coming at you, and this is not your advantage, nor anybody else's disadvantage; it is your seeing spreading its wings to encompass the full consequences of all the possibilities that are making themselves available to you.

When you see events like this, you are peering into linear existence from a multidimensional perspective. That is one of the ways that wisdom is arrived upon. When you say you don't understand, this shows you where you are trapped within your own syntactical version of yourself.

You keep repeating to yourself that you are not powerful enough to grasp or apply what I have been teaching you, but again, you are wrong. That is the predatorial consciousness speaking on behalf of your true self. You have confined yourself in a socially-determined version of who you are, and you need to drop it to progress. Remember, you are living out your predetermined destiny right at this very moment. Zero in on the truths of that, and remember to endeavor to stop talking to yourself.

Although you have made up your mind that my stories are too vast for you to comprehend, you are engaged in something so immense and diverse, and its right in front of your eyes. Live through your own experience, for that is the real seat of your power. Your potential is being reflected back at you at every single moment.

Your power is right in the palm of your hand. All you have to do is look around and realize that you are doing the exact thing that I am, in comparison to your own capacity. I am merely leveraging you to realize that your true potential is within reach. The holographic universe is at your disposal. All you have to do is clear out the socially-determined conditioning that has been impressed upon you.

Realize that you are nothing and you will become everything.

In the end we are the sum total of our doings and we will be faced by those doings at the moment of our death. Or is it our death in every moment that we live that faces us with what we do?

Lujan Matus

EPILOGUE

One of the most important practices we can apply ourselves to is developing our awareness of union. I have provided a technique here, called 'The Mirror', as a foundation to initiate this refined aspect of consciousness. This is one of the practices featured in 'Awakening the Third Eye', which you can find at www.parallelperception.com.

Through gazing upon the world with the intention to merge, we avail ourself to our true sensitivities, within and without. In this way we begin to cultivate those qualities necessary for our appropriate progression. Whatever you gaze at gazes back at you. Within this exchange you will always find yourself inwardly reflected. This is your heart of hearts, calling and responding to itself. When you listen to the song of a beautiful bird, when you truly listen, you hear yourself singing.

THE MIRROR

'The Mirror' is an essential preliminary practice to bring awareness into alignment with the intention of gazing. This is the state of consciousness I was subject to when my attention was redeployed by the masterful acts of my benefactors. As I viewed the complexity that was my compartmentalization in terms of my third eye capacity, I was taught this technique.

Imagine that you are laying your right hand upon your chest, over your heart center, and choose an object to gaze at. Any will do. Simultaneously view the object while immersed in the feeling of your heart. Realize that as you see it, it sees you.

Everything you encounter, be aware of the perception that merges with you. You are everything and everything is you, in terms of the feeling that presses from your heart, through your eyes, to what you gaze at. Be immersed within the union that is ever present, that we have been isolated from by virtue of the fact that our individuality gives us the illusion of separation.

Next, when you meet another human being, view them as you view yourself, while you are immersed in your own heartfelt feelings. This will bring you into a point of union.

Listen to them intently, giving them your full attention, your wholeheartedness. Watch every gesture that emerges. Be careful not to become fixated, even though you are concentrated. Be without effort. Keep a light heart. Do not seek to speak of what you discover. Only listen and watch the event unfold. This is the first step away from the obsessive self. Do not seek personal validation at any point. Do not add any part of yourself.

Practice this awareness for at least twenty-one days, until it becomes you. Be of service to those you encounter. Do what they ask of you without quarrel, without question.

Become aware of your bindings, your conditioned programming, through this practice. Remember do not speak out of turn. Watch and be kind.

Love or honor the other that you are gazing upon as if they were you. Give your time to them as if their time was your time to be given.

Do not regret any of your actions and do not seek any form of validation. Do not display any gestures that may reveal the way you feel, if you are being offended. Keep it to yourself.

Grab yourself a diary and write down all the opposing forces and feelings that you have that erupt within you. Do not write about the other person, for in this instance they are you, in terms of the activity you have undertaken.

Move slowly and carefully, gently away from everything. This act within itself will merge and unify you, separating that part of yourself that may be selfish into units that can be examined for recall. Though this may seem contradictory, in doing this you will begin to become aware of those isolated elements that actually are preventing you from being whole.

The Mirror technique has been employed for centuries to bring about the awareness of ascension, thus connecting the initiate with the presence of eternity in every moment that is continually escaping us.

2599956R00130

Made in the USA
San Bernardino, CA
10 May 2013